DOCTOR FAUSTUS

Also from Routledge:

ROUTLEDGE · ENGLISH · TEXTS

GENERAL EDITOR · JOHN DRAKAKIS

Doctor Faustus

by Christopher Marlowe

Edited by
JOHN D. JUMP

London and New York

This edition first published 1965
by Metheun & Co. Ltd
Reprinted 1968
Reprinted 1969 twice

Reprinted 1970 by Methuen Educational Ltd
Reprinted twelve times

Reprinted 1988 (twice), 1994, 1995
by Routledge
11 New Fetter Lane, London EC4P 4EE
29 West 35th Street, New York, NY 10001

ISBN 0 415 03960 6

Introduction and Notes © John D. Jump 1965

Printed in Great Britain by
J. W. Arrowsmith Ltd, Bristol

Contents

Preface

The text of *Doctor Faustus* printed here reproduces exactly that printed in my 'Revels' edition of the play, published by Methuen in 1962. But, in view of the special needs of the readers for whom the present volume is intended, the editorial apparatus of introduction, notes, etc. is very largely new.

All textual notes have been omitted; so, too, have the alternative versions of five scenes which differ too widely from the accepted versions for their variants to be digestible into textual notes and which were therefore printed in full in an appendix to the 'Revels' edition. The long textual sections of the earlier introduction have been replaced by a very brief account of the characteristic features of my text of the play.

For section 8 of the present introduction, I have borrowed at length from my critical discussion and interpretation of *Doctor Faustus* in section 9 of its predecessor and have expanded what I have borrowed. Otherwise, the present introduction owes little to the earlier one. It incorporates a modern-spelling version of the passages from the source-book which were previously given, with the original spelling and punctuation, in an appendix.

The notes have been greatly increased in bulk, despite the omission from them of all discussions of merely textual points and nearly all literary, historical, and other materials not serving a directly elucidatory purpose. In deciding which of them should be printed as footnotes and which should appear at the end of the volume, I have tried to bear in mind the reader's convenience. The footnotes contain brief explanations of most of the single words and short phrases that seem likely to cause difficulty. Words and phrases that call for fuller explanation than is suitable in a footnote, longer phrases, and all proper names are dealt with in the notes that follow the text of the play. In these more discursive notes, I have also elucidated various historical references and allusions to special bodies of knowledge, commented occasionally upon grammatical and stylistic features of the dialogue, and related the action of the play to the theatre in which it was originally performed.

7

In preparing this edition, I have incurred debts which it is a pleasure to acknowledge. Mr John Prudhoe of the Department of Drama in the University of Manchester very kindly read what I had written about Marlowe's theatre and gave me the benefit of his criticism and advice; Dr R. F. Leslie of the Department of English in the same university read what I had written about the morality plays and discussed a number of points of Elizabethan grammar with me in an equally helpful spirit; and Miss Tatiana A. Wolff of the Loughton County High School very generously allowed me to reproduce the time-chart which she had compiled for her edition of *Tamburlaine* and to revise it slightly in order to relate it more closely to *Doctor Faustus*. I am most grateful to all of them.

JOHN D. JUMP

Manchester, 1964

Chronology of Marlowe's Life and Works

(Adapted from a time-chart compiled by Tatiana A. Wolff)

1564   Christopher Marlowe born in Canterbury. His father, John, was a shoemaker, a member of the shoemakers' and tanners' guild.

        Shakespeare and Galileo born; Michelangelo and Calvin died.

1570   *The Pope excommunicated Queen Elizabeth I.*

1571   *Battle of Lepanto.*

1572   *Massacre of St Bartholomew.*

1576   *The Theatre, later re-erected as the Globe (1599), built in Holywell, Shoreditch, by James Burbage. The Lord Admiral's company of players already in existence.*

1577   *Two new theatres opened: the Blackfriars and the Curtain in Shoreditch.*

1579   Marlowe recorded as receiving a grant of £1 a quarter at the King's School, Canterbury.

1580   Marlowe entered Corpus Christi College, Cambridge. He is recorded in his first week to have paid the sum of 1*d.* at the buttery.

        Drake returned from his voyage round the world. Spenser was appointed secretary to Lord Grey de Wilton, who was going to Ireland as Lord Deputy.

1581   *Ralegh returned to England from Ireland and rose to favour at court.*

1582   *Plague in London. Hakluyt's* Divers Voyages touching the Discovery of America *published.*

1583   *Queen's company of players formed.*

1584   Marlowe took his B.A. degree.
        Ralegh organized expedition to explore Virginia.

1585   *Expedition to the Netherlands under Leicester. Parma captured Antwerp after a long siege.*

1586   *Battle of Zutphen, at which Sir Philip Sidney was killed.*

1587   Marlowe took his M.A. degree. *Tamburlaine the Great,* Parts I and II, performed in London.
        Execution of Mary, Queen of Scots. Drake's expedition to Cadiz. Ralegh made captain of the Queen's guard. The Rose theatre built in Southwark. Kyd's Spanish Tragedy *performed about this time. The German Faust-Book published.*

1588   *Defeat of the Spanish Armada.*

1589   *The Jew of Malta* performed. Marlowe imprisoned in New-gate for taking part in a street fight. Tried at the Old Bailey and discharged.
        Hakluyt's Principal Navigations, Voyages, and Dis-coveries of the English Nation *published. Ralegh in Ireland, met Spenser and persuaded him to bring his manuscript of* The Faerie Queene *to London.*

1590   *Tamburlaine the Great,* Parts I and II, published.
        Spenser's Faerie Queene, Books I–III, *published.*

1591   *Shakespeare's* Henry VI, Parts II and III, *performed.*

1592   *Edward II* performed. *Doctor Faustus* performed (probably 1592–3; but 1588 and 1589 are also possible).
        Siege of Rouen, in which the English helped the Protes-tants against the Catholic League. Plague in London; theatres closed. Ralegh imprisoned in the Tower on ac-count of his secret marriage to Elizabeth Throckmorton. Shakespeare's Henry VI, *Part I, performed. P.F.'s translation of the German Faust-Book published.*

1593   *The Massacre at Paris* performed. *Hero and Leander* written.
        Shakespeare's Venus and Adonis *published. Churchgoing enforced in England on pain of banishment; fresh dis-abilities imposed on recusants. Plague in London; theatres closed from February.*

12 *May*   Thomas Kyd arrested. Under torture he later said that certain heretical documents denying the divinity of

Christ, which had been found in his possession, belonged to Marlowe, with whom he had shared a room two years earlier.

18 *May* Warrant issued for Marlowe's arrest.

30 *May* Marlowe stabbed to death in a tavern brawl at Deptford. He and Ingram Frizer, who killed him, had quarrelled about the payment of the reckoning.

1 *June* Christopher Marlowe buried, in the churchyard of St Nicholas at Deptford.

1594 *The Tragedy of Dido, Queen of Carthage*, written in collaboration with Thomas Nashe, published. *Edward II* published.

1595 *The Swan theatre built.*

1598 *Hero and Leander* published in two editions, one incomplete as Marlowe left the poem, the other finished by George Chapman.

1599 'The Passionate Shepherd to his Love' published in an anthology, *The Passionate Pilgrim*, falsely attributed to Shakespeare. Printed copies of Marlowe's translations from Ovid's *Amores* publicly burnt by order of the Archbishop of Canterbury and the Bishop of London, on the ground of their licentiousness.

The opening of the Globe theatre on the Bankside, built from the timbers of the demolished Theatre.

1600 Marlowe's translation of Lucan's *Pharsalia*, Book I, published.

The Fortune theatre in Cripplegate opened by Henslowe and Alleyn.

1604 *Doctor Faustus* published in a shortened form (the A-version).

1616 *Doctor Faustus* published in a fuller form (the B-version).

(Owing to a lack of evidence, many events in Elizabethan literary and theatrical history cannot be dated with certainty. In such instances, the dates given above are those which seem likeliest in the present state of our knowledge.)

Introduction

I. ORIGINS OF THE FAUSTUS LEGEND

During the first millennium of the Christian era, a number of stories developed concerning men who were supposed to have acquired supernatural gifts or powers by making agreements with the Devil. One of the earliest and most widespread of these legends told of a bishop's seneschal named Theophilus who, in the reign of the Emperor Justinian, was wrongfully dismissed from his office. In his resentment, he sealed a contract renouncing Jesus Christ and the Virgin Mary and acknowledging Satan as his lord. His restoration to his office followed immediately. But Theophilus soon became terrified at what he had done. For forty nights he fasted and prayed to the Virgin; at last she appeared and listened to his plea. Reassured of the divine mercy, he made a public confession of his sin and proclaimed the miracle of his preservation. The contract was burned, and Theophilus shortly afterwards died in a state of grace, becoming known as Theophilus the Penitent. His story is representative of many, for interest in the theme persisted throughout the Middle Ages.

In the sixteenth century, a new leading character emerged, who was to become more famous than Theophilus or any other of his predecessors. The age was that of the wandering scholars, the disseminators of the New Learning, men who were masters and practitioners of many arts and who were often popularly suspected of sorcery. Belief in magic and witchcraft seems to have infected the very air of the sixteenth and seventeenth centuries. Conditions were such that one of these strolling scholars, a German, became the nucleus around which there crystallized a whole body of legend and folk-lore related to the notion of a compact with the Evil One.

The historical George or John Faustus seems to have been an itinerant scholar and fortune-teller. Documents alluding to his activities bear dates from 1507 to the later 1530's. Another dated 1545 mentions that he had died not long before. These documents do not compose a very attractive portrait. One of them tells us that as a schoolmaster Faustus had been guilty of the grossest immorality and that he had had to take flight from punishment; two of them refer to his arrogance and boastfulness.

A work published by a Protestant theologian in 1548 was the first to ascribe to him a definite association with the supernatural powers of evil and a death at the hands of the Devil. A fuller description of this terrible death followed in 1562. During the subsequent quarter-century, the legend underwent further elaboration. In 1572, a translation of a work which had been published two years earlier on the Continent made Faustus' name known to English readers. Then, in 1587, there appeared the first full and consecutive narrative of the legendary life and death of this new leading character in the old tale of the compact with Satan.

This, the work of an anonymous Protestant, was published in Frankfurt-on-Main as the *Historia von D. Iohañ Fausten* and may be conveniently referred to as the German Faust-Book. A translation of its title-page will give a very fair idea of its scope and tendency: 'History of Dr. John Faust, the celebrated conjuror and master of black magic: How he sold himself to the Devil with effect from an appointed time: What in the meanwhile were the strange adventures he witnessed, himself initiated, and conducted, until at last he received his well-deserved reward. Mostly collected and printed from his own writings which he left behind him, as a terrifying instance and horrible example, and as a friendly warning to all arrogant, insolent-minded, and godless men.' The motto is taken from James iv, 7: 'Submit yourselves therefore to God. Resist the devil, and he will flee from you.'

The German Faust-Book aims above all at edification. It shows the awful consequences of a sinner's deliberate commitment of himself to evil with a view to gratifying his pride, ambition, and lust. At the same time, the historical Faustus had been a wandering scholar, and even his moralistic biographer was affected by the characteristic influences of his time. So the German Faust-Book allows its hero some slight touches of the Renaissance intellectual curiosity. The century was also that of the Reformation. So it was easy enough for the legend to acquire a markedly anti-papal bias.

2. THE FIRST ENGLISH BIOGRAPHY OF FAUSTUS

A translation into English followed within five years. It bore the title, *The History of the Damnable Life and Deserved Death of Doctor John Faustus*; its author was a 'gentleman' known to us by his initials alone, P.F. Elizabethan translators normally took appreciable liberties with their originals, and P.F. was no exception. His independence is strikingly evident in his chapter xxii, which corresponds with chapter xxvi in the German Faust-Book. In each version, this chapter describes Faustus' world-wide travels. But the *Damnable Life*'s narrative contains details which do not occur in the German Faust-Book's. The German makes no mention of Virgil's tomb, but P.F. says, 'There saw he the tomb of Virgil, and the highway that he cut through that mighty hill of stone in one night, the whole length of an English mile.' After following his original in referring to the famous Piazza in Venice, P.F. on his own responsibility describes 'the sumptuous church standing therein, called St Mark's; how all the pavement was set with coloured stones, and all the rood or loft of the church double gilded over'. In the same way, he amplifies the account of Rome by introducing the four bridges over the Tiber, upon one of which 'is the castle of St Angelo, wherein are so many great cast pieces as there are days in a year'.

The insertions quoted here are of particular interest because each of them is unquestionably the source of a passage in Marlowe's play. Reviewing his travels, Faustus says in viii, 13–20:

> There saw we learned Maro's golden tomb,
> The way he cut, an English mile in length,
> Thorough a rock of stone in one night's space.
> From thence to Venice, Padua, and the rest,
> In midst of which a sumptuous temple stands,
> That threats the stars with her aspiring top,
> Whose frame is pav'd with sundry colour'd stones
> And roof'd aloft with curious work in gold.

Describing Rome, where they have just arrived, Mephostophilis speaks of the Tiber in viii, 37–44:

> Over the which four stately bridges lean,
> That make safe passage to each part of Rome.
> Upon the bridge call'd Ponte Angelo
> Erected is a castle passing strong,
> Where thou shalt see such store of ordinance
> As that the double cannons forg'd of brass
> Do match the number of the days contain'd
> Within the compass of one complete year.

This perfunctory versifying does not represent Marlowe at his best; but it is of importance here because his close adherence to the very wording of the *Damnable Life* in places where P.F. had no German original proves that he used P.F.'s translation in writing *Doctor Faustus*. Nor is other evidence hard to find. The articles of Faustus' compact with Lucifer as given in scene v of the play agree with P.F.'s version in that the fourth of them represents a conflation of the fourth and fifth articles of the German original; whereas the German author makes Faustus blow in the Pope's face, the playwright in scene ix follows P.F. in making him smite the Pope on the face; and in the same scene the playwright takes over from P.F. the addition to the Pope's curse of 'bell, book, and candle'.

Did he perhaps use the German version as well as P.F.'s ? There is no need to suppose so. Not one significant instance has been found of the play's agreeing with the German version when the English translation disagrees with it. We may safely assume that *Doctor Faustus* derives from the *Damnable Life*, and that everything that it owes to the German Faust-Book has reached it through the agency of P.F.

P.F.'s own contribution to the legend went beyond the supplying of additional detail to the record of Faustus' sightseeing. He also gave a distinctly stronger emphasis to the intellectual ardour of his hero. We must be careful not to exaggerate here. P.F. was, after all, a translator, and the tale he tells is in the main that told in his original. But the German gave him no authority, for example, for allowing Faustus in chapter xxii to describe himself as 'the unsatiable speculator'. By touches of this kind, P.F. was contributing to Faustus' development into the representative Renaissance figure that he was to become in Marlowe's play.

The use made in the play of the materials taken from the *Damn-*

able Life varied widely from place to place. Occasionally, a few words sufficed to suggest a whole episode, such as Faustus' conference with Valdes and Cornelius in scene i; at other times, as when Faustus meets the Duke and Duchess of Vanholt in scene xvii, the very phrases of P.F. are faithfully echoed. Only a few scenes of clownage, and the passages concerning the rivalry of Pope Adrian and the antipope, Bruno, appear to owe nothing to this source. A scene-by-scene presentation of the passages which appear to have contributed to the composition of *Doctor Faustus* will help to make this varying relationship clear.

3. EXTRACTS FROM THE *Damnable Life*

Doctor Faustus, Prologue, 11–27. (A narrative of Faustus' life up to the time when the play opens.)

Damnable Life, i. John Faustus, born in the town of Rhode, lying in the province of Weimar in Germany, his father a poor husbandman and not able well to bring him up; but having an uncle at Wittenberg, a rich man and without issue, took this J. Faustus from his father and made him his heir; insomuch that his father was no more troubled with him, for he remained with his uncle at Wittenberg, where he was kept at the university in the same city to study divinity. But Faustus, being of a naughty mind and otherwise addicted, applied not his studies but took himself to other exercises. . . He gave himself secretly to study necromancy and conjuration, insomuch that few or none could perceive his profession.

But to the purpose: Faustus continued at study in the university and was by the rectors and sixteen masters afterwards examined how he had profited in his studies; and being found by them that none for his time were able to argue with him in divinity, or for the excellency of his wisdom to compare with him, with one consent they made him Doctor of Divinity.

Damnable Life, ii. You have heard before that all Faustus' mind was set to study the arts of necromancy and conjuration, the which exercise he followed day and night; and, taking to him the wings of an eagle, thought to fly over the whole world, and to know the secrets of heaven and earth. For his speculation was so wonderful, being expert in using his *vocabula*, figures, characters, conjurations, and other ceremonial actions.

Doctor Faustus, i. (Faustus rejects the traditional subjects of study and turns to magic; he confers with Valdes and Cornelius.)

Damnable Life, i. Doctor Faustus . . . fell into such fantasies and deep cogitations that he was marked of many . . . and sometime he would throw the Scriptures from him as though he had no care of his former profession. . . He accompanied himself with divers that were seen in those devilish arts, and that had the Chaldean, Persian, Hebrew, Arabian, and Greek tongues, using figures, characters, conjurations, incantations, with many other ceremonies belonging to these infernal arts . . . insomuch that he could not abide to be called Doctor of Divinity but waxed a worldly man and named himself an astrologian . . . and for a shadow sometimes a physician and did great cures.

Doctor Faustus, iii, 1–37. (Faustus invokes Mephostophilis.)

Damnable Life, ii. And, taking his way to a thick wood near to Wittenberg, called in the German tongue *Spisser Waldt*, that is in English the Spissers Wood (as Faustus would oftentimes boast of it among his crew, being in his jollity), he came into the same wood towards evening into a cross-way, where he made with a wand a circle in the dust, and within that many more circles and characters. And thus he passed away the time, until it was nine or ten of the clock in the night. Then began Doctor Faustus to call for Mephostophiles the spirit and to charge him in the name of Beelzebub to appear there personally without any long stay. . . Faustus all this while, half amazed at the devil's so long tarrying, and doubting whether he were best to abide any more such horrible conjurings, thought to leave his circle and depart; whereupon the devil made him such music of all sorts as if the nymphs themselves had been in place; whereat Faustus was revived and stood stoutly in his circle aspecting his purpose, and began again to conjure the spirit Mephostophiles in the name of the prince of devils to appear in his likeness. Whereat suddenly over his head hanged hovering in the air a mighty dragon. . . Presently not three fathom above his head fell a flame in manner of a lightning and changed itself into a globe. . . Suddenly the globe opened and sprang up in height of a man; so, burning a time, in the end it converted to the shape of a fiery man. This pleasant beast ran about the circle a great while, and lastly appeared in manner of a gray friar, asking Faustus what was his request.

Doctor Faustus, iii, 38–44 and 95–99. (Faustus states his demands.)

Damnable Life, iii. Then began Doctor Faustus anew with him to conjure him that he should be obedient unto him, and to answer him certain articles, and to fulfil them in all points:

1. That the spirit should serve him and be obedient unto him in all things that he asked of him from that hour until the hour of his death.

2. Farther, anything that he desired of him he should bring it to him.

3. Also, that in all Faustus his demands or interrogations the spirit should tell him nothing but that which is true.

Hereupon the spirit answered and laid his case forth, that he had no such power of himself until he had first given his prince (that was ruler over him) to understand thereof and to know if he could obtain so much of his lord: 'Therefore speak farther, that I may do thy whole desire to my prince, for it is not in my power to fulfil without his leave.'

Doctor Faustus, iii, 65–75. (Faustus asks Mephostophilis about Lucifer and his fall.)

Damnable Life, x. Here Faustus said, 'But how came thy lord and master Lucifer to have so great a fall from heaven?' Mephostophiles answered, 'My lord Lucifer was a fair angel, created of God as immortal, and being placed in the seraphins, which are above the cherubins, he would have presumed unto the throne of God, with intent to have thrust God out of his seat. Upon this presumption, the Lord cast him down headlong, and, where before he was an angel of light, now dwells he in darkness.'

Damnable Life, xiii. 'My lord Lucifer (so called now, for that he was banished out of the clear light of heaven) was at the first an angel of God. He sat on the cherubins and saw all the wonderful works of God. Yea, he was so of God ordained, for shape, pomp, authority, worthiness, and dwelling, that he far exceeded all other the creatures of God. . . But when he began to be high-minded, proud, and so presumptuous that he would usurp the seat of his majesty, then was he banished out from amongst the heavenly powers.'

Doctor Faustus, v, 31–115. (Despite the congealing of his blood and the warning, '*Homo fuge!*' Faustus signs the bond.)

Damnable Life, iv. This swift-flying spirit appeared to Faustus, offering himself with all submission to his service, with full authority from his prince to do whatsoever he would request, if so be Faustus would promise to be his. . . Doctor Faustus gave him this answer, though faintly (for his soul's sake), That his request was none other but to become a devil, or at the least a limb of him, and that the spirit should agree unto these articles as followeth:

1. That he might be a spirit in shape and quality.

2. That Mephostophiles should be his servant and at his commandment.

3. That Mephostophiles should bring him anything and do for him whatsoever.

4. That at all times he should be in his house, invisible to all men except only to himself, and at his commandment to show himself.

5. Lastly, that Mephostophiles should at all times appear at his command, in what form or shape soever he would.

Upon these points, the spirit answered Doctor Faustus that all this should be granted him and fulfilled, and more, if he would agree unto him upon certain articles as followeth:

First, that Doctor Faustus should give himself to his lord Lucifer, body and soul.

Secondly, for confirmation of the same, he should make him a writing, written with his own blood.

Thirdly, that he would be an enemy to all Christian people.

Fourthly, that he would deny his Christian belief.

Fifthly, that he let not any man change his opinion, if so be any man should go about to dissuade or withdraw him from it.

Damnable Life, v. To confirm it the more assuredly, he took a small penknife and pricked a vein in his left hand; and for certainty thereupon were seen on his hand these words written, as if they had been written with blood, *O homo fuge*; whereat the spirit vanished. But Faustus continued in his damnable mind and made his writing as followeth.

Damnable Life, vi. *How Doctor Faustus set his blood in a saucer on warm ashes and writ as followeth.* . . 'Now have I, Doctor John Faustus, unto the hellish prince of orient and his messenger Mephostophiles given both body and soul, upon such condition, that they shall learn me and fulfil my desire in all things, as they have promised and vowed unto me, with due obedience unto me, according unto the articles mentioned between us.

'Further, I covenant and grant with them by these presents that, at the end of twenty-four years next ensuing the date of this present letter, they being expired, and I in the meantime during the said years be served of them at my will, they accomplishing my desires to the full in all points as we are agreed, that then I give them full power to do with me at their pleasure, to rule, to send, fetch, or carry me or mine, be it either body, soul, flesh, blood, or goods, into their habitation, be it wheresoever.'

Doctor Faustus, v, 116–27. (Faustus questions Mephostophilis about hell.)

Damnable Life, xi. *How Doctor Faustus . . . questioned with his spirit of matters as concerning hell, with the spirit's answer . . .* 'My Mephostophiles, I pray thee resolve me in this doubt. What is hell ? what substance is it of ? in what place stands it ? and when was it made ?' Mephostophiles answered, 'My Faustus, thou shalt know that before the fall of my lord Lucifer there was no hell; but even then was hell ordained. It is of no substance, but a confused thing. . . In this confused hell is nought to find but a filthy, sulphurish, fiery, stinking mist or fog. Further, we devils know not what substance it is of, but a confused thing. . . But to be short with thee, Faustus, we know that hell hath neither bottom nor end.'

Doctor Faustus, v, 141–79. (Mephostophilis refuses Faustus a wife; he gives him a book of charms.)

Damnable Life, ix. Doctor Faustus . . . , bethinking himself of a wife, called Mephostophiles to counsel, which would in no wise agree, demanding of him if he would break the covenant made with him, or if he had forgot it. 'Hast not thou,' quoth Mephostophiles, 'sworn thyself an enemy to God and all creatures ? To this I answer thee thou canst not marry. Thou canst not serve two masters, God and my prince; for wedlock is a chief institution ordained of God, and that hast thou promised to defy, as we do all, and that hast thou also done, and moreover thou hast confirmed it with thy blood. Persuade thyself that what thou dost in contempt of wedlock, it is all to thine own delight. Therefore, Faustus, look well about thee and bethink thyself better, and I wish thee to change thy mind; for, if thou keep not what thou hast promised in thy writing, we will tear thee in pieces like the dust under thy feet. Therefore, sweet Faustus, think with what unquiet life, anger, strife, and debate thou shalt live in, when thou takest a wife. Therefore change thy mind.' . . .

Then Faustus said unto him, 'I am not able to resist nor bridle my fantasy. I must and will have a wife, and I pray thee give thy consent to it.' . . . Hereupon appeared unto him an ugly devil, so fearful and monstrous to behold that Faustus durst not look on him. The devil said, 'What wouldst thou have, Faustus ? How likest thou thy wedding ? What mind art thou in now ?' Faustus answered, he had forgot his promise, desiring him of pardon and he would talk no more of such things. The devil answered, 'Thou were best so to do,' and so vanished.

After appeared unto him his friar Mephostophiles with a bell in his hand and spake to Faustus: 'It is no jesting with us. Hold thou that which thou hast vowed, and we will perform as we have promised; and, more than that, thou shalt have thy heart's desire of what woman soever thou wilt, be she alive or dead, and so long as thou wilt thou shalt keep her by thee.'

Damnable Life, x. Mephostophiles . . . brought with him a book in his hand of all manner of devilish and enchanted arts, the which he gave Faustus, saying, 'Hold, my Faustus, work now thy heart's desire.'

Doctor Faustus, vi, 1–105 and 172–80. (Faustus questions Mephostophilis about astronomy. The devils combat his efforts to repent by showing him 'some pastime', and Mephostophilis promises him a tour of hell.)

Damnable Life, xviii. Doctor Faustus . . . called unto him Mephostophiles his spirit, saying . . . , 'When I confer *Astronomia* and *Astrologia*, as the mathematicians and ancient writers have left in memory, I find them to vary and very much to disagree. Wherefore I pray thee to teach me the truth in this matter.'

Damnable Life, xix. *How Doctor Faustus fell into despair with himself; for, having put forth a question unto his spirit, they fell at variance, whereupon the whole rout of devils appeared unto him, threatening him sharply*. Doctor Faustus . . . became so woeful and sorrowful in his cogitations that he thought himself already frying in the hottest flames of hell. . . [Mephostophiles said,] 'Although I am not bound unto thee in such respects as concern the hurt of our kingdom, yet was I always willing to answer thee.'. . . Faustus . . . spake in this sort: 'Mephostophiles, tell me how and after what sort God made the world.'. . . The spirit, hearing this, answered, 'Faustus, thou knowest that all this is in vain for thee to ask.'. . . Whereat Faustus, all sorrowful for that he had put forth such a question, fell to weeping and to howling bitterly. . . And . . . the greatest devil in hell appeared unto him, with certain of his hideous and infernal company in the most ugliest shapes that it was possible to think upon, and . . . spake in this sort: 'Faustus, I have seen thy thoughts, which are not as thou hast vowed unto me by virtue of this letter,' and showed him the obligation that he had written with his own blood, 'wherefore I am come to visit thee and to show thee some of our hellish pastimes.'. . . Saith Faustus, 'I will that thou teach me to transform myself in like sort as thou and the rest have done.' Then Lucifer put forth his paw and gave Faustus a book, saying, 'Hold, do what thou wilt.'

Damnable Life, xx. Quoth Faustus, 'I would know of thee if I may see hell and take a view thereof.' 'That thou shalt,' said the devil, 'and at midnight I will fetch thee.'

Doctor Faustus, Cho. 1, 1-14. (An account of Faustus' space-travels.)

Damnable Life, xxi. [From a letter of Faustus to a friend.] 'I, being once laid on my bed, and could not sleep for thinking on my calendar and practice, I marvelled with myself how it were possible that the firmament should be known and so largely written of men, or whether they write true or false, by their own opinions or supposition or by due observations and true course of the heavens. Behold, being in these my muses, suddenly I heard . . . a groaning voice which said, 'Get up, the desire of thy heart, mind, and thought shalt thou see.'. . . And behold, there stood a waggon, with two dragons before it to draw the same, and all the waggon was of a light burning fire. . . I got me into the waggon, so that the dragons carried me upright into the air. . . On the Tuesday went I out, and on Tuesday seven-nights following I came home again, that is, eight days. . . And like as I showed before . . . even so the firmament, wherein the sun and the rest of the planets are fixed, moved, turned, and carried with the wind, breath, or spirit of God, for the heavens and firmament are moveable as the chaos, but the sun is fixed in the firmament. . . I was thus nigh the heavens, where methought every planet was but as half the earth . . . and methought that the whole length of the earth was not a span long.'

Doctor Faustus, viii, 1-46. (Faustus travels to Rome.)

Damnable Life, xxii. He took a little rest at home, and, burning in desire to see more at large and to behold the secrets of each king-

dom, he set forward again on his journey upon his swift hors‹
Mephostophiles and came to Trier, for that he chiefly desired to
see this town and the monuments thereof. But there he saw not
many wonders, except one fair palace that belonged unto the
bishop, and also a mighty large castle that was built of brick, with
three walls and three great trenches, so strong that it was impossible for any prince's power to win it. . . From whence he departed
to Paris, where he liked well the academy; and what place or kingdom soever fell in his mind, the same he visited. He came from
Paris to Mainz, where the river of Main falls into the Rhine. Notwithstanding, he tarried not long there but went to Campania in
the kingdom of Neapolis, in which he saw an innumerable sort of
cloisters, nunneries, and churches, great and high houses of stone,
the streets fair and large and straight forth from one end of the
town to the other as a line; and all the pavement of the city was of
brick, and the more it rained in the town the fairer the streets were.
There saw he the tomb of Virgil, and the highway that he cut
through that mighty hill of stone in one night, the whole length of
an English mile. . . From thence he came to Venice, whereas he
wondered not a little to see a city so famously built standing in the
sea. . . He wondered not a little at the fairness of St Mark's place
and the sumptuous church standing therein, called St Mark's;
how all the pavement was set with coloured stones, and all the rood
or loft of the church double gilded over. Leaving this, he came to
Padua. . . Well, forward he went to Rome, which lay, and doth yet
lie, on the river Tybris, the which divideth the city in two parts.
Over the river are four great stone bridges, and upon the one bridge
called *Ponte S. Angelo* is the castle of St Angelo, wherein are so
many great cast pieces as there are days in a year, and such pieces
that will shoot seven bullets off with one fire. . . Hard by . . . he
visited the churchyard of St Peter's, where he saw the pyramid
that Julius Caesar brought out of Africa.

Doctor Faustus, ix, 55–112. (Faustus breaks up the Pope's banquet
and is formally cursed.)

Damnable Life, xxii. Amongst the rest, he was desirous to see the
Pope's palace and his manner of service at his table; wherefore he
and his spirit made themselves invisible and came into the Pope's
court and privy chamber, where he was. There saw he many servants attending on his Holiness, with many a flattering sycophant
carrying of his meat; and there he marked the Pope and the manner

of his service, which he seeing to be so unmeasurable and sumptuous, 'Fie,' quoth Faustus, 'why had not the devil made a pope
of me ?'. . . On a time the Pope would have a feast prepared for the
Cardinal of Pavia, and for his first welcome the Cardinal was bid-
den to dinner; and, as he sat at meat, the Pope would ever be blessing and crossing over his mouth. Faustus could suffer it no longer,
but up with his fist and smote the Pope on the face, and withal he
laughed that the whole house might hear him, yet none of them
saw him nor knew where he was. The Pope persuaded his company
that it was a damned soul, commanding a mass presently to be said
for his delivery out of purgatory, which was done. The Pope sat
still at meat. But, when the latter mess came in to the Pope's board,
Doctor Faustus laid hands thereon, saying, 'This is mine.' And so
he took both dish and meat and fled unto the Capitol or *Campi-
doglio*, calling his spirit unto him, and said, 'Come, let us be merry,
for thou must fetch me some wine and the cup that the Pope drinks
of.'. . . But, when the Pope and the rest of his crew perceived they
were robbed, and knew not after what sort, they persuaded themselves that it was the damned soul that before had vexed the Pope
so and that smote him on the face; wherefore he sent commandment through all the whole city of Rome that they should say mass
in every church, and ring all the bells for to lay the walking spirit,
and to curse him with bell, book, and candle that so invisibly had
misused the Pope's Holiness, with the Cardinal of Pavia and the
rest of their company.

Doctor Faustus, xii, 1–69. (Faustus makes Alexander the Great
appear before the Emperor Charles V.)

Damnable Life, xxix. The Emperor Carolus, the fifth of that name,
was personally with the rest of his nobles and gentlemen at the
town of Innsbruck, where he kept his court; unto the which also
Doctor Faustus resorted, and, being there well known of divers
nobles and gentlemen, he was invited into the court to meat, even
in the presence of the Emperor. . . The Emperor held his peace
until he had taken his repast; after which he called unto him
Faustus into the privy chamber; whither being come, he said unto
him, 'Faustus, I have heard much of thee; that thou art excellent
in the black art, and none like thee in mine empire. For men say
that thou hast a familiar spirit with thee, and that thou canst do
what thou list. It is, therefore,' saith the Emperor, 'my request of
thee that thou let me see a proof of thine experience; and I vow

unto thee, by the honour of mine imperial crown, none evil shall happen unto thee for so doing.' Hereupon Doctor Faustus answered his Majesty that upon those conditions he was ready, in anything that he could, to do his Highness' commandment in what service he would appoint him. 'Well, then hear what I say,' quoth the Emperor. 'Being once solitary in my house, I called to mind mine elders and ancestors; how it was possible for them to attain unto so great a degree of authority, yea, so high, that we the successors of that line are never able to come near. As for example the great and mighty monarch of the world Alexander Magnus was such a lantern and spectacle to all his successors, as the chronicles makes mention of so great riches, conquering and subduing so many kingdoms, the which I and those that follow me, I fear, shall never be able to attain unto. Wherefore, Faustus, my hearty desire is that thou wouldst vouchsafe to let me see that Alexander and his paramour, the which was praised to be so fair; and I pray thee show me them in such sort that I may see their personages, shape, gesture, and apparel, as they used in their lifetime, and that here before my face; to the end that I may say I have my long desire fulfilled, and to praise thee to be a famous man in thine art and experience.' Doctor Faustus answered, 'My most excellent lord, I am ready to accomplish your request in all things, so far forth as I and my spirit are able to perform. Yet your Majesty shall know, that their dead bodies are not able substantially to be brought before you; but such spirits as have seen Alexander and his paramour alive shall appear unto you in manner and form as they both lived in their most flourishing time; and herewith I hope to please your Imperial Majesty.' Then Faustus went a little aside to speak to his spirit; but he returned again presently, saying, 'Now, if it please your Majesty, you shall see them; yet upon this condition that you demand no question of them, nor speak unto them;' which the Emperor agreed unto. Wherewith Doctor Faustus opened the privy chamber door, where presently entered the great and mighty Emperor Alexander Magnus, in all things to look upon as if he had been alive . . . and so passing towards the Emperor Carolus he made low and reverent curtsy. Whereat the Emperor Carolus would have stood up to receive and greet him with the like reverence, but Faustus took hold of him and would not permit him to do it. Shortly after, Alexander made humble reverence and went out again and, coming to the door, his paramour met him, she coming in. She made the Emperor likewise reverence . . . The Emperor . . . said to himself, 'Now have I seen two persons, which my heart hath long wished for to behold; and sure it cannot otherwise be,' said he to himself, 'but that the spirits have changed themselves into these forms and have not deceived me.'. . . And, for that the Emperor would be the more satisfied in the matter, he thought, 'I have heard say that behind her neck she had a great wart or wen;' wherefore he took Faustus by the hand without any words and went to see if it were also to be seen on her or not; but she, perceiving that he came to her, bowed down her neck, where he saw a great wart; and hereupon she vanished, leaving the Emperor and the rest well contented.

Doctor Faustus, xii, 70–118. (Faustus has horns fixed on Benvolio's head.)

Damnable Life, xxx. When Doctor Faustus had accomplished the Emperor's desire in all things as he was requested, he went forth into a gallery and, leaning over a rail to look into the privy garden, he saw many of the Emperor's courtiers walking and talking together; and casting his eyes now this way, now that way, he espied a knight leaning out at a window of the great hall, who was fast asleep (for in those days it was hot); but the person shall be nameless that slept, for that he was a knight, although it was done to a little disgrace of the gentleman. It pleased Doctor Faustus, through the help of his spirit Mephostophiles, to firm upon his head as he slept an huge pair of hart's horns; and as the knight awaked, thinking to pull in his head, he hit his horns against the glass, that the panes thereof flew about his ears. Think here how this good gentleman was vexed, for he could neither get backward or forward; which when the Emperor heard all the courtiers laugh, and came forth to see what was happened, the Emperor also, when he beheld the knight with so fair a head, laughed heartily thereat and was therewithal well pleased. At last Faustus made him quit of his horns again; but the knight perceived how they came, etc.

Doctor Faustus, xiii, xiv. (Benvolio tries to obtain revenge.)

Damnable Life, xxxi. Doctor Faustus took his leave of the Emperor and the rest of the courtiers, at whose departure they were sorry, giving him many rewards and gifts. But, being a league and a half from the city, he came into a wood, where he beheld the knight that he had jested with at the court, with other in harness, mounted on fair palfreys and running with full charge towards Faustus. But he, seeing their intent, ran towards the bushes; and before he came amongst the bushes he returned again, running as it were to meet them that chased him; whereupon suddenly all the bushes were turned into horsemen, which also ran to encounter with the knight and his company, and, coming to them, they closed the knight and the rest and told them that they must pay their ransom before they departed. Whereupon the knight, seeing himself in such distress, besought Faustus to be good to them, which he denied not but let them loose. Yet he so charmed them that every one, knight and other, for the space of a whole month did wear a pair of goat's horns on their brows, and every palfrey a pair of ox-horns on their head; and this was their penance appointed by Faustus, etc.

Damnable Life, lii. Doctor Faustus travelled towards Eisleben, and when he was nigh half the way he espied seven horsemen, and the chief of them he knew to be the knight to whom he had played a jest in the Emperor's court, for he had set a huge pair of hart's horns upon his head. And, when the knight now saw that he had fit opportunity to be revenged of Faustus, he ran upon him himself, and those that were with him, to mischief him, intending privily to shoot at him; which when Doctor Faustus espied, he vanished away into the wood which was hard by them. But, when the knight perceived that he was vanished away, he caused his men to stand still, where, as they remained, they heard all manner of warlike instruments of music, as drums, flutes, trumpets, and such like, and a certain troop of horsemen running towards them. Then they turned another way, and there also were assaulted on the same side; then another way, and yet they were freshly assaulted; so that, which way soever they turned themselves, he was encountered; insomuch that when the knight perceived that he could escape no way, but that they his enemies laid on him which way soever he offered to fly, he took a good heart and ran amongst the thickest and thought with himself better to die than to live with so great an infamy. Therefore, being at handy-blows with them, he demanded the cause why they should so use them. But none of them would give him answer, until Doctor Faustus showed himself unto the knight, wherewithal they enclosed him round, and Doctor Faustus said unto him, 'Sir, yield your weapon, and yourself; otherwise it will go hardly with you.' The knight, that knew none other but that he was environed with an host of men (where indeed they were none other than devils), yielded. Then Faustus took away his sword, his piece and horse, with all the rest of his companions. And further he said unto him, 'Sir, the chief general of our army hath commanded to deal with you according to the law of arms; you shall depart in peace whither you please.' And then he gave the knight an horse after the manner and set him thereon. So he rode; the rest went on foot until they came to their inn, where, being alighted, his page rode on his horse to the water, and presently the horse vanished away, the page being almost sunk and drowned. But he escaped; and, coming home, the knight perceived his page so bemired and on foot, asked where his horse was become; who answered that he was vanished away. Which when the knight heard, he said, 'Of a truth, this is Faustus his doing, for he serveth me now as he did before at the court, only to make me a scorn and a laughing-stock.'

Doctor Faustus, xv. (Faustus tricks a Horse-courser.)

Damnable Life, xxxiv. In like manner he served an horse-courser at a fair, called Pheiffring. For Doctor Faustus through his cunning had gotten an excellent fair horse, whereupon he rid to the fair, where he had many chapmen that offered him money. Lastly, he sold him for forty dollars, willing him that bought him, that in any wise he should not ride him over any water. But the horse-courser marvelled with himself that Faustus bade him ride him over no water; 'but,' quoth he, 'I will prove;' and forthwith he rid him into the river. Presently the horse vanished from under him, and he sat on a bundle of straw, insomuch that the man was almost drowned. The horse-courser knew well where he lay that had sold him his horse; wherefore he went angerly to his inn, where he found Doctor Faustus fast asleep and snorting on a bed. But the horse-courser could no longer forbear him, took him by the leg, and began to pull him off the bed; but he pulled him so, that he pulled his leg from his body, insomuch that the horse-courser fell down backwards in the place. Then began Doctor Faustus to cry with an open throat, 'He hath murdered me!' Hereat the horse-courser was afraid and gave the flight, thinking none other with himself but that he had pulled his leg from his body. By this means Doctor Faustus kept his money.

Doctor Faustus, xvi, 18–30. (Faustus eats a whole load of hay.)

Damnable Life, xxxv. Doctor Faustus being in a town of Germany called Zwickau, where he was accompanied with many doctors and masters, and going forth to walk after supper, they met with a clown that drove a load of hay. 'Good even, good fellow,' said

Faustus to the clown; 'what shall I give thee to let me eat my belly-ful of hay?' The clown thought with himself, 'What a madman is this to eat hay!' Thought he with himself, 'Thou wilt not eat much.' They agreed for three farthings he should eat as much as he could. Wherefore Doctor Faustus began to eat, and that so ravenously that all the rest of his company fell a-laughing, blinding so the poor clown that he was sorry at his heart, for he seemed to have eaten more than the half of his hay. Wherefore the clown began to speak him fair, for fear he should have eaten the other half also. Faustus made as though he had had pity on the clown and went his way. When the clown came in place where he would be, he had his hay again as he had before, a full load.

Doctor Faustus, xvii, 1–8. (Faustus entertains the Duke of Vanholt with an 'enchanted castle'.)

Damnable Life, xl. Doctor Faustus desired the Duke of Anholt to walk a little forth of the court with him. Wherefore they went both together into the field, where Doctor Faustus through his skill had placed a mighty castle; which, when the Duke saw, he wondered thereat, so did the Duchess and all the beholders, that on that hill, which was called the Rohumbuel, should on the sudden be so fair a castle. . . But as they were in their palace they looked towards the castle, and behold it was all in a flame of fire. . . And thus the castle burned and consumed away clean. Which done, Doctor Faustus returned to the Duke, who gave him great thanks for showing them of so great courtesy.

Doctor Faustus, xvii, 8–35. (Faustus produces grapes in winter for the Duchess of Vanholt.)

Damnable Life, xxxix. Doctor Faustus on a time came to the Duke of Anholt, the which welcomed him very courteously. This was in the month of January, where, sitting at the table, he perceived the Duchess to be with child and, forbearing himself until the meat was taken from the table and that they brought in the banqueting dishes, said Doctor Faustus to the Duchess, 'Gracious lady, I have alway heard that the great-bellied women do always long for some dainties. I beseech therefore your Grace hide not your mind from me, but tell me what you desire to eat.' She answered him, 'Doctor Faustus, now truly I will not hide from you what my heart doth most desire, namely, that if it were now harvest I would eat my bellyful of ripe grapes and other dainty fruit.' Doctor Faustus answered hereupon, 'Gracious lady, this is a small thing for me to do, for I can do more than this.' Wherefore he took a plate and made open one of the casements of the window, holding it forth, where incontinent he had his dish full of all manner of fruits, as red and white grapes, pears, and apples, the which came from out of strange countries. All these he presented the Duchess, saying, 'Madam, I pray you vouchsafe to taste of this dainty fruit, the which came from a far country, for there the summer is not yet ended.' The Duchess thanked Faustus highly, and she fell to her fruit with full appetite. The Duke of Anholt notwithstanding could not withhold to ask Faustus with what reason there were such young fruit to be had at that time of the year. Doctor Faustus told him, 'May it please your Grace to understand that the year is divided into two circles over the whole world; that, when with us it is winter, in the contrary circle it is notwithstanding summer; for in India and Saba there falleth or setteth the sun, so that it is so warm that they have twice a year fruit. And, gracious lord, I have a swift spirit, the which can in the twinkling of an eye fulfil my desire in anything; wherefore I sent him into those countries, who hath brought this fruit as you see.' Whereat the Duke was in great admiration.

Doctor Faustus, xvii, 106–16. (Faustus silences the obstreperous clowns.)

Damnable Life, xxxvii. Doctor Faustus went into an inn, wherein were many tables full of clowns, the which were tippling can after can of excellent wine, and, to be short, they were all drunken, and as they sat they so sung and hallowed that one could not hear a man speak for them. This angered Doctor Faustus; wherefore he . . . so conjured them that their mouths stood as wide open as it was possible for them to hold them, and never a one of them was able to close his mouth again.

Doctor Faustus, xviii, 1–9. (Faustus makes his will and feasts with the students.)

Damnable Life, lvi. And, when the time drew nigh that Faustus should end, he called unto him a notary and certain masters the which were his friends and often conversant with him, in whose presence he gave this Wagner his house and garden. Item, he gave him in ready money 1600 guilders. Item, a farm. Item, a gold chain, much plate, and other household stuff. This gave he all to his servant, and the rest of his time he meant to spend in inns and students' company, drinking and eating, with other jollity. And thus he finished his will for that time.

Doctor Faustus, xviii, 10–37. (Faustus makes Helen of Troy appear to the students.)

Damnable Life, xlv. The Sunday following came these students home to Doctor Faustus his own house . . . and, being merry, they began some of them to talk of the beauty of women; and every one gave forth his verdict what he had seen and what he had heard. So one among the rest said, 'I never was so desirous of anything in this world as to have a sight, if it were possible, of fair Helena of Greece, for whom the worthy town of Troy was destroyed and razed down to the ground; therefore,' saith he, 'that in all men's judgement she was more than commonly fair, because that when she was stolen away from her husband there was for her recovery so great bloodshed.'

Doctor Faustus answered: 'For that you are all my friends and are so desirous to see that famous pearl of Greece, fair Helena, the wife of King Menelaus, and daughter of Tindalus and Leda, sister to Castor and Pollux, who was the fairest lady in all Greece, I will therefore bring her into your presence personally, and in the same form of attire as she used to go when she was in her chiefest flowers and pleasantest prime of youth. . . I charge you all that upon your perils you speak not a word.'. . . And so he went out of the hall, returning presently again; after whom immediately followed the fair and beautiful Helena, whose beauty was such that the students were all amazed to see her, esteeming her rather to be a heavenly than an earthly creature.

Doctor Faustus, xviii, 38–83. (An Old Man tries to save Faustus.)

Damnable Life, xlviii. A good Christian, an honest and virtuous old man, a lover of the holy Scriptures, who was neighbour unto Doctor Faustus . . . began with these words . . . : 'My good neighbour, you know in the beginning how that you have defied God and all the host of heaven and given your soul to the devil, wherewith you have incurred God's high displeasure and are become from a Christian far worse than a heathen person. Oh, consider what you have done. It is not only the pleasure of the body but the safety of the soul that you must have respect unto; of which if you be careless, then are you cast away and shall remain in the anger of almighty God. But yet is it time enough, Doctor Faustus, if you repent and call unto the Lord for mercy. . . Let my words, good brother Faustus, pierce into your adamant heart; and desire God, for his son Christ his sake, to forgive you.'. . . All this while Doctor Faustus heard him very attentively, and replied, 'Father, your persuasions like me wondrous well, and I thank you with all my heart for your goodwill and counsel, promising you so far as I may to follow your discipline.' Whereupon he took his leave. And being come home he laid him very pensive on his bed, bethinking himself of the words of the good old man, and in a manner began to repent that he had given his soul to the devil, intending to deny all that he had promised unto Lucifer. Continuing in these cogitations, suddenly his spirit appeared unto him, clapping him upon the head, and wrung it as though he would have pulled the head from the shoulders, saying unto him, 'Thou knowest, Faustus, that thou hast given thyself body and soul unto my lord Lucifer and hast vowed thyself an enemy unto God and unto all men; and now thou beginnest to hearken to an old doting fool, which persuadeth thee as it were unto God, when indeed it is too late, for that thou art the devil's, and he hath good power presently to fetch thee. Wherefore he hath sent me unto thee to tell thee that, seeing thou hast sorrowed for that thou hast done, begin again and write another writing with thine own blood. If not, then will I tear thee all to pieces.' Hereat Doctor Faustus was sore afraid and said, 'My Mephostophiles, I will write again what thou wilt.' Wherefore he sat him down, and with his own blood he wrote as followeth.

Doctor Faustus, xviii, 90–118. (Faustus becomes Helen's lover.)

Damnable Life, lv. To the end that this miserable Faustus might fill the lust of his flesh and live in all manner of voluptuous pleasures, it came in his mind after he had slept his first sleep, and in the twenty-third year past of his time, that he had a great desire to lie with fair Helena of Greece, especially her whom he had seen and showed unto the students of Wittenberg. Wherefore he called unto him his spirit Mephostophiles, commanding him to bring him the fair Helena, which he also did. Whereupon he fell in love with her and made her his common concubine and bedfellow; for she was so beautiful and delightful a piece that he could not be one hour from her if he should therefore have suffered death.

Doctor Faustus, xviii, 84–9 and 119–27. (On Faustus' orders, Mephostophilis tries to torment the Old Man.)

> *Damnable Life*, xlix. And presently . . . he became so great an enemy unto the poor old man that he sought his life by all means possible. But this godly man was strong in the Holy Ghost, that he could not be vanquished by any means. . . And when he [Mephostophiles] came home Faustus asked him how he had sped with the old man; to whom the spirit answered, the old man was harnessed, and that he could not once lay hold upon him.

Doctor Faustus, xix, 24–86. (Faustus converses with the Scholars on the night before the twenty-four years have expired.)

> *Damnable Life*, lxiii. 'My trusty and well-beloved friends, the cause why I have invited you into this place is this: Forasmuch as you have known me this many years, in what manner of life I have lived, practising all manner of conjurations and wicked exercises, the which I have obtained through the help of the devil . . . I have promised unto him at the end and accomplishing of twenty-four years both body and soul, to do therewith at his pleasure. And this day, this dismal day, those twenty-four years are fully expired; for, night beginning, my hour-glass is at an end, the direful finishing whereof I carefully expect. For out of all doubt this night he will fetch me, to whom I have given myself in recompense of his service, both body and soul, and twice confirmed writings with my proper blood. . . And, I beseech you, let this my lamentable end to the residue of your lives be a sufficient warning that you have God always before your eyes, praying unto him that he would ever defend you from the temptation of the devil, and all his false deceits; not falling altogether from God, as I wretched and ungodly damned creature have done, having denied and defied baptism, the sacraments of Christ's body, God himself, all heavenly powers and earthly men – yea, I have denied such a God that desireth not to have one lost. . . Lastly, to knit up my troubled oration, this is my friendly request, that you would to rest, and let nothing trouble you. Also, if you chance to hear any noise or rumbling about the house, be not therewith afraid, for there shall no evil happen unto you. Also I pray you arise not out of your beds.'. . .
>
> One of them said unto him, 'Ah, friend Faustus, what have you done to conceal this matter so long from us ? We would by the help of good divines, and the grace of God, have brought you out of

this net and have torn you out of the bondage and chains of Satan; whereas now we fear it is too late, to the utter ruin of your body and soul.' Doctor Faustus answered, 'I durst never do it, although I often minded to settle myself unto godly people, to desire counsel and help. . . Yet when I was minded to amend . . . then came the devil and would have had me away, as this night he is like to do, and said so soon as I turned again to God he would dispatch me altogether.'. . . But, when the students heard his words, they gave him counsel to do naught else but call upon God, desiring him for the love of his sweet son Jesus Christ's sake to have mercy upon him.

Doctor Faustus, xix, 133–90. (Faustus' final soliloquy.)

Damnable Life, lix. This sorrowful time drawing near so troubled Doctor Faustus that he began to write his mind . . . as followeth:
   'Ah, Faustus, thou sorrowful and woeful man, now must thou go to the damned company in unquenchable fire, whereas thou mightest have had the joyful immortality of the soul, the which thou now hast lost.'

Damnable Life, lx. 'Oh, poor, woeful, and weary wretch! Oh, sorrowful soul of Faustus, now art thou in the number of the damned; for now must I wait for unmeasurable pains of death, yea, far more lamentable than ever yet any creature hath suffered . . . Ah, grievous pains that pierce my panting heart; whom is there now that can deliver me? Would God that I knew where to hide me or into what place to creep or fly! Ah, woe, woe is me; be where I will, yet am I taken.'

Damnable Life, lxi. 'Now thou, Faustus, damned wretch, how happy wert thou if as an unreasonable beast thou mightest die without soul, so shouldst thou not feel any more doubts! But now the devil will take thee away both body and soul and set thee in an unspeakable place of darkness. . . Ah, that I could carry the heavens on my shoulders, so that there were time at last to quit me of this everlasting damnation! Oh, who can deliver me out of these fearful tormenting flames, the which I see prepared for me? Oh, there is no help, nor any man that can deliver me, nor any wailing of sins can help me; neither is there rest to be found for me day nor night.'

Doctor Faustus, xx. (The Scholars discover Faustus' remains.)

Damnable Life, lxiii. When the gentlemen were laid in bed, none of them could sleep, for that they attended to hear if they might be privy of his end. It happened between twelve and one o'clock at midnight there blew a mighty storm of wind against the house, as though it would have blown the foundation thereof out of his place. Hereupon the students began to fear, and got out of their beds, comforting one another; but they would not stir out of the chamber; and the host of the house ran out of doors, thinking the house would fall. The students lay near unto that hall wherein Doctor Faustus lay, and they heard a mighty noise and hissing, as if the hall had been full of snakes and adders. With that the hall door flew open wherein Doctor Faustus was; then he began to cry for help, saying, 'Murder, murder!' But it came forth with half a voice hollowly; shortly after, they heard him no more. But when it was day, the students, that had taken no rest that night, arose and went into the hall in the which they left Doctor Faustus; where notwithstanding they found no Faustus; but all the hall lay besprinkled with blood, his brains cleaving to the wall; for the devil had beaten him from one wall against another; in one corner lay his eyes, in another his teeth, a pitiful and fearful sight to behold. Then began the students to bewail and weep for him and sought for his body in many places. Lastly they came into the yard where they found his body lying on the horse dung, most monstrously torn and fearful to behold; for his head and all his joints were dashed in pieces.

The forenamed students and masters that were at his death have obtained so much that they buried him in the village where he was so grievously tormented.

4. DATE OF THE PLAY

The earliest known copy of the *Damnable Life* was published in the latter half of 1592. There had probably been an earlier edition than that which it alone represents, but the evidence of a dispute in 1592 regarding the ownership of the copyright is such as to make it likely that this earlier edition had appeared as recently as in the spring of the same year. Marlowe was killed in May 1593. So it seems that, unless he had had access to the manuscript of the *Damnable Life*, he must have written *Doctor Faustus* during the twelve months or so prior to his death.

Since the 1930's, scholarly opinion has been growing more and more willing to accept this late date for the play. Previously, 1588 and 1589 were generally favoured; and there are still critics who cling to these early dates. Their more detailed arguments can find no place here. But, when they support their views by relating *Doctor Faustus* to Marlowe's whole development as a dramatist, they produce a case of more general interest, and perhaps of greater persuasiveness. Briefly, they argue that Marlowe's plays, taken in the order 1 and 2 *Tamburlaine*, *Doctor Faustus*, *The Jew of Malta*, and *Edward II*, illustrate a progressive decline of humanist faith. In 1 and 2 *Tamburlaine* Marlowe celebrates the aspiring mind; in *Doctor Faustus* he wavers; in *The Jew of Malta* his justification of individualism is cynical; in *Edward II* it is tired. Along with this change in outlook there goes an increasing sophistication of technique. The earlier plays are straightforward stagings of the life-histories of dominant protagonists; *The Jew of Malta* achieves a greater complexity of intrigue; finally, *Edward II* embodies a genuine dramatic conflict between two opposing groups of characters.

This is plausible, but it does not settle the matter. If the plays are taken in the order 1 and 2 *Tamburlaine*, *The Jew of Malta*, *Edward II*, and *Doctor Faustus*, they can be seen to illustrate an increasingly defiant assertion of individualism, followed by the eventual recognition of its necessary limitations. In 1 and 2 *Tamburlaine* Marlowe's aspiring hero is a glorious conqueror. Then, just as Graham Greene in *The Power and the Glory* challengingly focuses upon an unprepossessing representative of the priesthood he wishes to justify, so Marlowe in *The Jew of Malta* and *Edward II* focuses first upon a villainous and then upon a feeble and wilful exponent of the individualism he upholds. Finally, in *Doctor Faustus* he returns to a more admirable protagonist in order to express his continuing sympathy with the aspiring mind at the same time as he sadly recognizes that this must come to terms with realities both natural and supernatural if it is not to bring about its own downfall. As for the difference in structure between *Edward II* and the other plays, that is best explained by reference to the belief that Marlowe wrote these other plays for a company dominated by the great tragic actor, Edward Alleyn, whereas he wrote *Edward II* for a company in which talent was more equally distributed.

So the reader is free to place *Doctor Faustus* at any point he pleases in Marlowe's career subsequent to his completion of the second part of *Tamburlaine*. The more objective evidence does admittedly point to the later date, 1592-3. But it is not conclusive;

and the reader is in the happy position of knowing that, while his critical intuitions in favour of 1588 or 1589 or 1592-3 are too subjective to weigh very heavily as evidence with other people, nothing has yet emerged from the scholarly discussion of the date to prevent him from trusting them as far as he is himself concerned.

5. AUTHORSHIP OF THE PLAY

Was Marlowe the sole author of *Doctor Faustus*? Hardly anyone seems to think so. There is almost unanimous agreement that the scenes of clownage introducing such characters as Robin, Dick, and the Horse-courser, and the comic scenes at the papal, imperial, and ducal courts, are not from his hand. In the early scenes in which Faustus commits himself to evil, and in the late scenes in which he approaches and suffers destruction, the verse style is often unmistakably Marlowe's; and these same scenes contain a fair number of echoes of his other works. But if he wrote iii, 46-56, in which Mephostophilis carefully explains that Faustus' charms had no coercive power over him but merely attracted him to come voluntarily to one whose sinful state of mind they advertised, he can hardly have written x, 32-4, in which Mephostophilis protests that the charms recited by a couple of ignorant clowns have dragged him against his will all the way from Constantinople. A similar, though less clear-cut, discrepancy is that between the tragic Faustus, fluctuating between arrogance and remorse, whom Marlowe portrays, and the jaunty anti-papist wonder-worker and court entertainer who bears Faustus' name in the comic scenes. We must be careful not to exaggerate this discrepancy, however. During the period when he is revelling in his power, Faustus naturally exhibits traits different from those which are most prominent early and late in his career.

These inconsistencies are among the more palpable of the items of evidence supporting the division of the play between Marlowe and another along some such lines as those already indicated. The name of this other author is unknown, and no proposed identification has met with wide acceptance. There may even have been two others, one responsible for the scenes of clownage, the other for the comic scenes. The likeliest candidate for the authorship of the comic scenes is Samuel Rowley, an actor and playwright who died about 1633. But it is difficult either to establish or to overthrow a claim when there is only one play from which to deduce the claimant's characteristics as a dramatist, and that a play written no less than eleven or twelve years after the time when he might have contributed to *Doctor Faustus*.

It is conceivable that Samuel Rowley wrote the prose scenes of clownage, too. Thomas Nashe (1567–1601), the pamphleteer, has also been named in connection with them. But it seems wisest to admit that, after all our guess-work, we simply do not know who wrote them. Some playwrights of the period must have vanished without leaving a trace, and this may even have been one of them.

Marlowe, then, seems to have written all or most of the following: the Prologue; scenes i, iii, v, and vi; Chorus 1; the first four or five speeches of scene viii; Chorus 2; scenes xviii, xix, and xx; and the Epilogue. He may also have written scene ii. The rest of the play was evidently contributed mainly by his collaborator or collaborators. If there were two collaborators, one of them presumably wrote the farcical prose scenes, the other the comic scenes at the courts of Rome, Germany, and Vanholt.

Despite the differences in execution which permit us to discriminate between its Marlowan and its non-Marlowan parts, *Doctor Faustus* possesses a genuine unity of conception. This will be demonstrated in section 8. Most readers have felt that Marlowe's must have been the mind responsible for this conception; certainly, the theme of the play is highly characteristic of him. So much is this the case that we feel the work to be essentially his, even while we deny that he wrote more than a part of it. His collaborator or collaborators evidently subordinated themselves to him, working to a scenario for which he was mainly, or even entirely, responsible. We do them no great injury when we speak of *Doctor Faustus*, as we commonly do, as Marlowe's achievement.

6. THE RENAISSANCE

The age in which Marlowe conceived his play was the age which saw the full flowering of the Renaissance in England. This 'complex, many-sided movement' had begun in Italy two hundred years earlier; it had grown in strength and had spread; and early in the sixteenth century it had reached even the remote British Isles. Wherever its influence penetrated, great things were achieved in the arts, and especially in the arts of painting, sculpture, architecture, and poetry. In English literature, its representatives include Spenser, Bacon, Shakespeare, Donne, Jonson, and Milton. They include also Marlowe himself.

A number of distinguishable trends contributed to this 'many-sided but yet united movement' as a whole. First, there was the new learning. The humanists were reviving and extending classical studies and so making available to their fellows a wider range of knowledge and ideas; and printing, invented in the fifteenth century, helped greatly in the dissemination of the fresh materials. Under the influence of this new learning, there evolved the ideal of the cultivated Renaissance man in whom all the faculties were harmoniously developed, an ideal believed by Englishmen to have been realized by, for example, Sir Philip Sidney.

Second, there was the Reformation. This challenged the view that only as a member of the corporate body, the church, could the individual find salvation. The Protestants, in separating themselves from the Roman Catholic Church, tended to emphasize the individual's responsibility for finding salvation by reading and interpreting Scripture for himself. In England, the Anglican Church was attempting to take the middle way between Roman Catholic institutionalism and Protestant individualism.

Third, there was the discovery of new lands and new routes. Columbus discovered America; Vasco da Gama doubled the Cape of Good Hope and sailed to India; Magellan penetrated into the Pacific Ocean; and the first circumnavigations of the earth, including that of Sir Francis Drake, occurred. Such voyages had important economic and other practical consequences. In addition, they gave men the sense that in the physical world as in the world of ideas the boundaries of the known were being very rapidly enlarged.

Finally, exploration was proceeding beyond the earth itself. In place of the old view that the entire universe centred on a stationary earth, there was being elaborated the new view that the earth was only one among many planets travelling around the sun. Copernicus put forward this view in 1543, and Galileo, born in the same year as Marlowe and Shakespeare, brought the theory to the practical test of the telescope. It must not be thought that these discoveries had much effect even upon educated Elizabethans. Marlowe, for example, still thought of the universe, in the old Ptolemaic way, as centred on a stationary earth. Nevertheless, the new science was developing; and Bacon was to be one of its early philosophers.

As a whole, the general movement we call the Renaissance can be seen in a number of different ways. It can be seen as a revolt against the stable and ordered but restrictive world of the later Middle Ages. More positively, it can be seen as what Walter Pater, two of whose formulations on the subject have already been quoted, calls 'a general excitement and enlightening of the human mind'. This excitement found expression in a freely-ranging curiosity which tended to enlighten men both about themselves and about the world and the universe around them. It found expression also in the new individualism in conduct, philosophy, religion, and art, which is so prominent a feature of the age. Perhaps these three – an impulse towards emancipation, a spirit of inquiry, and an assertion of individualism – are the leading characteristics of the movement.

In *Doctor Faustus*, Marlowe placed a representative of it upon the English stage. We have already seen that P.F. allowed Faustus to call himself 'the unsatiable speculator' and that minute traces of the same Renaissance intellectual curiosity are visible even in the hero of the German Faust-Book. But such slight manifestations might easily have passed unnoticed if Marlowe's achievement had not alerted us to look for something of the kind in his predecessors. In the main, the author of the German Faust-Book and his English translator both aim at edifying their readers. Like other homilists, they are not above exploiting the sensational and the farcical possibilities of the tale they tell. But they have little sympathy with the aspirations which lead Faustus to conclude his compact, and they use his decline and fall simply to point a serious moral warning to their readers.

Marlowe, however, takes a much more complex attitude towards his material. His Faustus has the restless curiosity, the riotous imagination, and the audacious desires of a man responding fully and delightedly to the new trends in his age and the possibilities they seem to open up. Marlowe evidently feels a fervent sympathy with him. But his sympathy is far from unqualified. He makes it clear that Faustus is arrogant and headstrong and that the catastrophe is one that he wilfully brings about. The Marlowe who shows us this is no longer the simple rebel who wrote *Tamburlaine the Great*. Admittedly, rebellious impulses remain strong in him; but they are now opposed by the orthodox conviction that a sin of presumption or pride such as Faustus commits can only lead to destruction. Embodying the tension between these forces, *Doctor Faustus*, despite the unevenness of its execution, is indubitably Marlowe's greatest play; and this Renaissance play embodies the tension the more successfully because it is cast in a largely mediaeval mould.

7. THE MORALITY PLAYS

The mould in question was provided by the example of the morality plays. These grew out of the miracle plays, which were dramatizations of Bible stories. The moralities were presentations of Christian doctrine; their characters were personified abstractions linked in plots devised to point the necessary morals. The play *Mary Magdalene* illustrates a transitional stage in that it combines real characters, such as the saint herself and her father, brother, and sister, with allegorical personages, such as the Good and Bad Angels, the Seven Deadly Sins, and the World, the Flesh, and the Devil.

The earliest extant regular morality is the late fifteenth-century *Castle of Perseverance*. This follows the spiritual career of Humanum Genus, or Mankind, from his birth, through his often sinful life, to his death and his salvation by God's mercy. The forces of good and evil which contend for his soul are represented by personified abstractions, including those named already in connection with *Mary Magdalene*: the Good and Bad Angels, the Seven Deadly Sins, and the World, the Flesh, and the Devil. But the finest morality play is *Everyman*, also of the late fifteenth century. God sends Death to summon Everyman, who looks for a friend to accompany him on his unsought but obligatory journey. After being rejected by one after another of the persons and things he has valued in this world, he finds that only his Good Deeds can travel with him to the judgement-seat of God.

At their best, the moralities impress us by their simple, grave enunciation of important general truths. They can also exhibit a remarkable psychological subtlety. This does not manifest itself in the portrayal of individual real characters of great complexity, such as many of those of Shakespeare, Racine, and Ibsen, but in the presentation of general human experience by the interaction of personified abstractions. By such means, *Everyman* communicates very powerfully a desperately unwilling relinquishment of what has been valued in life, leading to a detached acquiescence in a transition that has to be made.

Morality plays continued to be performed throughout the sixteenth century. The tradition remained strong in Marlowe's lifetime, and he profited by it in writing *Doctor Faustus*. As we have seen, his attitude towards Faustus was ambivalent. In so far as he felt himself to belong to the new age, he endorsed the aspirations of this representative Renaissance man and devoted some of his most eloquent and elated verse to expressing them; in so far as he retained, or had recovered, an orthodox abhorrence of presumption or pride, he considered Faustus' course of action to be impious and finally self-defeating and employed the morality form to convey his judgement of it. Morality features are frequent in his play. Faustus is flanked by his Good and Bad Angels, like Humanum Genus in *The Castle of Perseverance*; he leagues himself with allegorical representatives of the forces of evil; he delights in a show of the Seven Deadly Sins; and he comes close to repentance when exhorted by an Old Man who might well be the personified abstraction Good Counsel. Moreover, the subject of the play is the central morality subject, the struggle between the forces of good and evil for the soul of man – in this case, of Renaissance man.

8. *The Tragical History of The Life and Death of Doctor Faustus*

The main action of *Doctor Faustus* divides conveniently into three parts. In the first, Faustus makes his decision and, after some hesitations and backward glances, commits himself to evil. Chorus 1 introduces the second part, in which Faustus exploits his dearly-bought power in Rome, in Germany, and in Vanholt. The third part extends from the opening of scene xviii to the Epilogue; it shows Faustus' behaviour as his end approaches and, as far as is practicable, it shows that end itself. Of these three parts, the second seems to contain very little writing by Marlowe; but the first and the third appear to be principally his.

1. Faustus commits himself to evil

The Chorus, or speaker of the Prologue, announces a play which differs from some that have recently been performed. This, he tells us, is not a play about ancient wars, or love in high places, or great deeds. It presents the career of a scholar, a man of humble origin who has acquired great learning. His arrogance will cause him to overreach and ruin himself. We are to witness a tragedy of presumption.

Presumption deeply interested and strongly attracted Marlowe. Not more than five years at the most before starting *Doctor Faustus*, he had placed in the mouth of his most-favoured protagonist, Tamburlaine, the assurance that Nature

> Doth teach us all to have aspiring minds.
> (1 *Tamburlaine*, II, vii, 20)

The attraction makes itself felt from the beginning of *Doctor Faustus*. In the first scene, Faustus reviews the traditional subjects of study, to which he has devoted himself so far. Philosophy, medicine, law, and divinity have come to seem mean and constricting to him. With impatient scorn he sweeps them aside; and with almost breathless eagerness he contemplates the

> world of profit and delight,
> Of power, of honour, of omnipotence
> (i, 52–3)

which he expects to enjoy as a magician. The whole earth, and the winds and clouds above it, will be subject to his control. While waiting for his friends Valdes and Cornelius, who are to instruct him in 'concealed arts' (i, 101), he swiftly reviews some of the widely varied uses to which he intends to put the skill he seeks. These testify to his ardent curiosity, his desire for luxury and wealth, and his nationalism, as well as to the longing for power which he has already voiced. Such qualities mark him unmistakably as a man of the Renaissance; and a whole series of allusions maintains throughout the scene our sense of the extended horizons of that age of discovery. Faustus craves for gold from the East Indies, for pearl from the depths of the ocean, and for 'pleasant fruits and princely delicates' (i, 84) from America; Valdes refers to the Indians in the Spanish colonies, to Lapland giants, to the argosies of Venice, and to the annual plate-fleet which supplied the Spanish treasury from the New World. There was much here to fire the imaginations of English theatregoers; and they would heartily approve of Faustus' determination to chase the Prince of Parma from the Netherlands. After all, only the defeat of the Spanish Armada had prevented Parma from invading England in 1588. Nor were Englishmen ignorant of 'the fiery keel at Antwerp's bridge' (i, 95). Its fame had spread far; and in 1588 its Italian inventor had been in the English service.

So Faustus' dream of power includes much that must by its nature have appealed strongly to the people for whom Marlowe wrote; and the liveliness and zest with which it is expounded must have made the appeal irresistible. After Faustus has sent for Valdes and Cornelius, he exclaims that he is 'glutted' (i, 77) with the notion of obtaining the power he avidly desires. He expects the spirits to gratify his senses, his understanding, and his will. 'I'll have them fly to India for gold' (i, 81), he promises himself; and eagerly and exultantly he lists the things that he will have them do. Each item or set of items in the catalogue is introduced by the assertive first personal pronoun: 'I'll have them read me strange philosophy. . . I'll have them wall all Germany with brass. . . I'll have them fill the public schools with silk. . . I'll levy soldiers with the coin they bring' (i, 85–91). These lines, with their identical openings, introduce the successive lyrical stanzas of from two to four lines each which compose the speech. But in the last of the stanzas Marlowe reverses the word-order; and so the rhapsody ends with one more assertive line of the kind that he has used to point the rhetorical structure throughout:

> Yea, stranger engines for the brunt of war
> Than was the fiery keel at Antwerp's bridge
> I'll make my servile spirits to invent.

(i, 94–6)

Valdes and Cornelius enter. Faustus' feverish enthusiasm again finds rhetorical utterance:

> Philosophy is odious and obscure,
> Both law and physic are for petty wits,
> Divinity is basest of the three,
> Unpleasant, harsh, contemptible, and vile;
> 'Tis magic, magic, that hath ravish'd me.

(i, 105–9)

This sentence, re-enacting the argument of his whole opening soliloquy, mounts to an enraptured climax at ''Tis magic, magic, that hath ravish'd me'. Ironically, we have here an echo of an earlier line, which voiced an orthodox academic admiration for Aristotle, 'Sweet Analytics, 'tis thou hast ravish'd me' (i, 6). The contrast shows how far Faustus has travelled.

Already we have reason for misgivings at the direction in which he is moving. His declaration,

> A sound magician is a demi-god,   (i, 61)

forces us to recognize the presumptuous nature of his ambition. He evidently aspires to be something more than a man. Without surprise, we learn that his conscience is uneasy. Not that he admits as much at this stage; but the internal conflict is externalized for us in the admonitions of his Good and Bad Angels. The first sentence of the Good Angel, a warning against incurring 'God's heavy wrath' (i, 71), crystallizes our fears for one who has much of our sympathy; and these fears are augmented when, in the following scene, the two Scholars perceive the 'danger of his soul' (ii, 31).

Faustus, however, persists in his chosen course. In scene iii, he succeeds in calling up Mephostophilis and proposes his bargain with Lucifer; in scene v, he signs his soul away to Lucifer and questions Mephostophilis about hell; in scene vi, he questions Mephostophilis about astronomy and is later entertained by an infernal show of the Seven Deadly Sins which is designed to distract him from thoughts of repentance.

But matters go less smoothly than this summary suggests. During these three scenes, Faustus suffers a number of rebuffs. Having performed the ritual by which, he believes, 'the spirits are enforc'd to rise' (iii, 13), he naturally regards the appearance of Mephostophilis as a proof that he can order him about. He proceeds to do so with a quite absurd arrogance. Mephostophilis disillusions him. Faustus' charms, he explains, did not oblige him to come; they merely drew his attention to Faustus' attractively sinful frame of mind, and he came of his own accord, 'in hope to get his glorious soul' (iii, 51). In scene v, after the signature of the bond, Faustus asks for a wife. Marriage is a sacrament, however; so Mephostophilis cannot give him one. Moreover, Faustus' presumption is already separating him from his fellow-men and making him incapable of marriage as a human relationship. So Mephostophilis' reply takes the form of a crude practical joke, followed by a promise of concubines galore. In scene vi, when Faustus questions him about astronomy, Mephostophilis tells him nothing that Wagner, the student who is his servant, could not have told him; and, when Faustus asks who made the world, Mephostophilis, reluctant to acknowledge the Creator, refuses to say. His refusal provokes a crisis in their relationship.

Anyone less infatuated than Faustus might have inferred from these rebuffs that the power he was acquiring so presumptuously fell far short of the 'omnipotence' (i, 53) of which he had dreamed. Faustus, however, brings himself to disregard not only these checks but also several quite explicit warnings. Of these, the most obvious is provided by the congealing of his blood, and its forming the words '*Homo fuge*' (v, 77), when he is busy signing the bond with it. Comparison with the *Damnable Life* shows how much Marlowe himself developed and emphasized this warning. Even Lucifer's grotesque show of the Seven Deadly Sins, with Pride appropriately at their head, can be seen as potentially admonitory in effect, whatever may have been the impresario's intention and Faustus' actual response to the performance. But the most eloquent warnings come from that melancholy, sombre, tortured, and surprisingly truthful fiend, Mephostophilis himself. Within fifty lines of their first meet-

ing, Faustus asks him what caused the fall of Lucifer. Mephostophilis ascribes it correctly to 'aspiring pride and insolence' (iii, 70),
that is, to factors such as are visible in Faustus himself. 'And what
are you', inquires Faustus, 'that live with Lucifer?'

> MEPH. Unhappy spirits that fell with Lucifer,
>   Conspir'd against our God with Lucifer,
>   And are for ever damn'd with Lucifer.
> FAU. Where are you damn'd?
> MEPH.   In hell.
> FAU. How comes it then that thou art out of hell?
> MEPH. Why, this is hell, nor am I out of it.
>   Think'st thou that I, who saw the face of God
>   And tasted the eternal joys of heaven,
>   Am not tormented with ten thousand hells
>   In being depriv'd of everlasting bliss?
>
> (iii, 72–82)

Mephostophilis, no doubt, means only to voice his own anguish.
But his words, which echo, unexpectedly enough, an utterance of
one of the Fathers of the church, would have conveyed a warning
if Faustus had been capable of receiving one. It is the same after
the signing of the bond in scene v. Faustus asks where hell is.
Mephostophilis first locates it in the centre of the sublunary, elemental part of the universe, then goes on to speak of it, as he did
in scene iii, as the spiritual condition of those who are entirely
separated from God:

> Hell hath no limits, nor is circumscrib'd
> In one self place, but where we are is hell,
> And where hell is, there must we ever be;
> And, to be short, when all the world dissolves
> And every creature shall be purify'd,
> All places shall be hell that is not heaven.
> FAU. I think hell's a fable.
> MEPH. Ay, think so still, till experience change thy mind.
>
> (v, 122–9)

Faustus does not merely neglect these warnings. He sweeps them
aside with impatient, flippant arrogance. When his blood congeals

to prevent his signing away his soul, he asks himself indignantly: 'is not thy soul thine own?' (v, 68). Admittedly, the injunction '*Homo fuge*' shakes his complacency for a moment. But he receives the Seven Deadly Sins with unreflecting jocularity; and in his glib and insensitive retorts to Mephostophilis' sombre speeches about hell he boastfully asserts his human self-sufficiency. To the first, he replies:

> What, is great Mephostophilis so passionate
> For being deprived of the joys of heaven?
> Learn thou of Faustus manly fortitude
> And scorn those joys thou never shalt possess.
>
> (iii, 85–8)

In response to the second, he denies the existence of hell.

> MEPH. But I am an instance to prove the contrary,
> For I tell thee I am damn'd and now in hell.
> FAU. Nay, and this be hell, I'll willingly be damn'd:
> What, sleeping, eating, walking, and disputing!
>
> (v, 137–40)

Faustus, then, concludes an infamous bargain in order to enjoy the knowledge, the pleasure, and above all the power for which he craves. In scene i we felt considerable sympathy and even admiration for him. Our reservations become greater and greater as the play proceeds and his swallowing-down of rebuffs and refusals, together with his frivolous dismissal of one warning after another, exposes the inordinate appetite which dominates him. He is wilful, headstrong, and blind.

His bargain requires him to abjure God. As early as in the original evocation of Mephostophilis, he is fully prepared to do this. At the beginning, he feels few misgivings. Indeed, scene iii ends with a further expression of the kind of elation which characterized him in scene i. If he had 'as many souls as there be stars', he would 'give them all for Mephostophilis' (iii, 104–5). But shortly before signing the bond he wavers. Again the Good and Bad Angels appear and externalize his internal struggle with his conscience. 'Contrition, prayer, repentance', which could reconcile him with God, are denounced by the Bad Angel as 'illusions, fruits of lunacy' (v, 17-19). Such doctrine helps Faustus to silence the voice of conscience. Once more he achieves the heady elation of scene i,

> Why, the signory of Emden shall be mine,   (v, 24)

but not before he has glimpsed a further temptation – to 'despair' (v, 4).

This temptation recurs momentarily when he first sees the words '*Homo fuge*'. It confronts him in full strength, however, at the beginning of scene vi. The Bad Angel then assures the man who has abjured God that he is beyond the reach of the divine mercy. Faustus confesses that his heart is hardened, that his conviction of his own damnation prevents him from repenting, and that he has thought of suicide:

> And long ere this I should have done the deed
> Had not sweet pleasure conquer'd deep despair.
>
> > (vi, 24-5)

But fifty lines later after Mephostophilis' refusal to say who made the world, Faustus comes near to achieving repentance. The two Angels appear, and for the first and last time it is the Good Angel who has the final word. Faustus is listening, and words of prayer begin to pass his lips. At this crisis, Mephostophilis invokes the aid of Lucifer and Beelzebub. They intimidate Faustus and, as soon as he again abjures God, 'gratify' (vi, 103) him with the show of the Seven Deadly Sins.

It is clear from this scene that the legalistic deed of gift which Lucifer required Faustus to sign is not really binding – in other words, that his initial sin has not damned him once and for all. The utterances of the Good and Bad Angels on their two appearances would be pointless if it were not still possible for Faustus to repent and by so doing to cancel the bond; and the emergency measures taken by Mephostophilis show that he certainly recognizes the possibility. 'For although . . . [Faustus] had made . . . [Satan] a promise, yet he might have remembered through true repentance sinners come again into the favour of God' (*Damnable Life*, xiii). In fact, the deed is validated from minute to minute only by Faustus' persistent refusal to relinquish such power as he has acquired by his presumption.

2. Faustus exploits his power

Faustus, then, abjuring God in the hope of becoming something more than a man, succeeds in fact in separating himself from God, isolating himself in large measure from his fellows, and consigning himself to the hell so powerfully suggested by Mephostophilis in scenes iii and v. Repentance remains possible; he represses yet another spontaneous impulse towards it as late as in scene xv. But it is unlikely to develop in one so lacking in humility and so greedy for the satisfactions, incomplete though they tend to be, which his sin brings him.

Incomplete they are indeed in comparison with what he felt able to promise himself in scene i. From scene viii to scene xvii, we watch him exploit his dearly-bought power. He goes on the rampage in the Vatican; he intervenes, effectively but inconclusively, in the strife between the Pope and the Emperor; he conjures for Charles V and revenges himself on a heckler; when the heckler retaliates, he takes a second revenge; he conjures for the Duke and Duchess of Vanholt; he tricks a horse-dealer; and, when the horse-dealer retaliates, he takes his revenge on him, too. For the 'world of profit and delight' which these escapades represent, Faustus voluntarily barters his soul.

Admittedly, these passages seem to be mainly the work of Marlowe's collaborator; and the change of authorship no doubt accounts for the temporary transformation of Faustus from an ambitious but sometimes fearful sinner into a brisk pope-baiter and practical joker. But we are entitled to assume that the authors were writing to an agreed scenario, drafted perhaps by Marlowe himself. If they were, they presumably wished us to see that Faustus had made an even worse bargain than had at first appeared; and they presumably meant the rebuffs and refusals which Faustus endures, as already described, in scenes iii, v, and vi to prepare us for this perception. The collaborator had no great talent, however, and produced a Faustus who is a poor substitute for Marlowe's. The verse at his command was alone enough, in all probability, to stop him from doing much better than he did. Its prim, earnest formality is emphasized by his taste for antitheses, for rhymes, and for proverbs and other stereotyped expressions. It completely lacks the impetus and splendour of Marlowe's verse. Even so, the purpose

embodied in the scenario to which the authors worked is still trace-
able in the plan of *Doctor Faustus*.

Whether it was the same collaborator or another who wrote the
farcical prose scenes which occur at intervals in the first two parts
of the play, they are even less worthy than are the comic scenes of
a place in the tragedy as conceived by Marlowe and alongside the
great scenes which he contributed to it. Naturally, topics which are
important in the more serious scenes tend to be echoed in the farcical scenes. Wagner, for example, asserts that Robin 'would give his
soul to the devil for a shoulder of mutton' (iv, 9–10); and in scene x
Robin conjures up an irate Mephostophilis. No doubt there is a
touch of crude burlesque in such places. But some recent critics
go further and claim to discern in them a profound, subtle, and
sustained irony such as that which, for example, links Falstaff's
famous speech on honour in I *Henry IV* with the more extravagant
utterances on the same subject by Harry Hotspur and others concerned in the main political action of the drama. For most of us,
however, the comparison with the Falstaff scenes in I *Henry IV* is
quite enough to dispel any notion that the farcical scenes in *Doctor
Faustus* are finely integrated into the thematic structure of the play
as a whole. The comparison serves also to bring out how undistin-
guished in themselves these farcical scenes are.

3. *The damnation of Faustus*

In the third part, we return to the heights. Faustus has already
suffered crises of conscience in scenes v, vi, and xv. One more crisis
of the kind occurs towards the end of the twenty-four years allowed
him in the deed of gift. In scene xviii, an Old Man exhorts him to
repent before it is too late:

> Though thou hast now offended like a man,
> Do not persever in it like a devil.
> Yet, yet, thou hast an amiable soul,
> If sin by custom grow not into nature:
> Then, Faustus, will repentance come too late,
> Then thou art banish'd from the sight of heaven;
> No mortal can express the pains of hell.
>
> (xviii, 41–7)

This good counsel has an immediate effect upon Faustus. But, since he lacks faith in God's mercy, the effect is merely to drive him towards despair.

> Damn'd art thou, Faustus, damn'd; despair and die!
> (xviii, 56)

Mephostophilis hands him a dagger, and only the Old Man's intervention and his assurance that God's mercy is still available prevent Faustus from stabbing himself. As he struggles to repent and fights against despair, he is subjected to the same treatment as proved so persuasive in scene vi. First, Mephostophilis terrifies him:

> Revolt, or I'll in piecemeal tear thy flesh; (xviii, 76)

then, when Faustus has submitted and has offered to renew the bond, he gratifies him with the 'sweet embraces' (xviii, 94) of Helen of Troy. Naturally, this is not Helen herself. Just as 'the royal shapes / Of Alexander and his paramour' (xii, 45–6) were presented by spirits, so Helen, too, is impersonated by a spirit; and Faustus in embracing her commits the sin of demoniality, or bodily intercourse with demons. The Old Man, learning this, concludes that he can now do nothing for Faustus; and by the next scene, his last, Faustus has finally added to his original presumption and abjuring of God the further mortal sin of despair.

Before he surrenders himself to Helen, Faustus utters his famous apostrophe, beginning:

> Was this the face that launch'd a thousand ships
> And burnt the topless towers of Ilium?
> Sweet Helen, make me immortal with a kiss.
> Her lips suck forth my soul: see where it flies!
> (xviii, 99–102)

Frequent allusions in Marlowe's works show that he had fed his imagination on the classical poetry and classical legend that men were studying so enthusiastically in the age of the Renaissance; and here, as already in ll. 23–32, he re-creates in highly evocative romantic terms the world of the *Iliad*. For this purpose he employs, perhaps for the last time, that formal, lyrical blank verse which he had developed in *Tamburlaine* and had used early in *Doctor Faustus*, as we have seen, to express the aspiration of his hero. He shapes the latter part of the speech into two stanzas, each consisting of three rhymeless couplets, and then adds a concluding unpaired line to take the full weight of the vow with which Faustus finally commits himself:

> I will be Paris, and for love of thee
> Instead of Troy shall Wittenberg be sack'd,
> And I will combat with weak Menelaus
> And wear thy colours on my plumed crest,
> Yea, I will wound Achilles in the heel
> And then return to Helen for a kiss.
> O, thou art fairer than the evening's air
> Clad in the beauty of a thousand stars,
> Brighter art thou than flaming Jupiter
> When he appear'd to hapless Semele,
> More lovely than the monarch of the sky
> In wanton Arethusa's azur'd arms,
> And none but thou shalt be my paramour.
>
> (xviii, 106–18)

Throughout this rhapsody we hear once more the note of elation which was so strong in the earlier scenes of the play; and the long-continued popularity of the speech apart from its context shows that readers have been able without misgivings to take it as expressing a simple, eager aspiration. But the speech is actually addressed to a fiend, who will indeed suck forth Faustus' soul; it is the immediate prelude to the sin which plunges him into irremediable despair; and its significance is underlined by the presence during most of it of the Old Man, whose comment becomes vocal at its close. Arousing these conflicting responses, the incident may reasonably be regarded as epitomizing the basic theme of the whole play.

By scene xix, then, Faustus has entirely lost hope. In a prose passage which must be one of the very few we have by Marlowe, he takes a moving farewell of the Scholars. Mephostophilis assures him that it is now too late to repent; and when the Angels enter immediately afterwards they merely moralize upon the fact of his damnation. For Faustus' conviction that he has committed himself finally to evil has made his despair absolute and impregnable. So what we hear in the great soliloquy which expresses his states of

mind and feeling during his last hour is the voice of an already
damned soul.

There is general agreement that this is Marlowe's most mature
passage of dramatic verse. It contrasts sharply not merely with the
set speeches in *Tamburlaine* but even with the apostrophe to Helen.
Whereas they are passages of more or less formal eloquence, this
develops flexibly, unpredictably, even disconcertingly. Shrinking
in terror, Faustus first addresses himself in a long series of mono-
syllables terminated emphatically by the polysyllable which focuses
his dread:

> Now hast thou but one bare hour to live,
> And then thou must be damn'd perpetually.
>
> (xix, 134–5)

He appeals for time, for

> A year, a month, a week, a natural day,   (xix, 140)

in which to repent, thus implicitly admitting that his deed of gift
did not make repentance impossible; and this appeal culminates
in his poignant quotation of a line of Latin verse. Ovid, whom he
quotes, wished to lengthen out the pleasure of the night; Faustus
wishes simply to defer the anguish of the morrow. The uselessness
of the appeal is conveyed in a two-line sentence which, starting with
an almost stately slowness, accelerates sharply to allude again to his
imminent damnation:

> The stars move still, time runs, the clock will strike,
> The devil will come, and Faustus must be damn'd.
>
> (xix, 143–4)

Even as late as this, he has an intimation of the divine mercy,
though it is now unattainable by him:

> See, see where Christ's blood streams in the firmament!
>
> (xix, 146)

and he seems to strain upwards in the broken alexandrine which immediately follows. Again he quails when tormented by the fiends;
and by calling desperately upon Lucifer to spare him he surrenders
himself afresh. His longing to hide himself from 'the heavy wrath
of God' (xix, 153) finds expression in Biblical terms such as themselves constitute a reminder that there can be no such concealment.

With the desperate cry, 'No, no' (xix, 154), he recognizes that there
is none.

Enough has been said to display something of the dramatic
urgency and widely varied expressiveness of this great monologue,
in which Faustus shows himself agonizingly aware of 'God's heavy
wrath', against which his Good Angel warned him in i, 71. Towards
its close, he forswears his humanism. Having prided himself on his
self-reliance, and having even striven to be more than a man, he
now longs to be less than a man; he wishes he could be 'a creature
wanting soul' (xix, 172), 'some brutish beast' (xix, 176), which at
death would face mere extinction and not eternal damnation. He
curses his parents for engendering him. No doubt the 'books' (xix,
190) which he offers to burn are primarily his books of magic. But
the word reminds us of his exclamation to the Scholars earlier in
the scene: 'O, would I had never seen Wittenberg, never read
book!' (xix, 45–6); and we retain the impression that Faustus is
ascribing his downfall in part to his learning. Hearing or reading
these concluding lines, and relating them to all that has preceded
them, we can surely have no hesitation in thinking of Faustus as
embodying the new inquiring and aspiring spirit of the age of the
Renaissance, and of Marlowe as expressing in this play both his
fervent sympathy with that new spirit and, ultimately, his awed
and pitiful recognition of the peril into which it could lead those
whom it dominated. Emancipation from an old order; the free play
of the mind; the assertion of one's individuality – these Renaissance purposes evidently attract Marlowe; but he delivers his last
word on the subject in the Epilogue, where he makes it clear that
'such forward wits' as 'practise more than heavenly power permits'
are preparing for themselves a 'hellish fall' (ll. 7–8, 4).

9. MARLOWE'S THEATRE

Doctor Faustus was written for performance. If, as we read, we are
to imagine for ourselves the kind of performance that the authors
envisaged when they wrote the play, we must imagine that performance as taking place in a typical Elizabethan theatre. No doubt
we should prefer to imagine it in the particular Elizabethan theatre
for which Marlowe wrote. But we do not know enough about that

particular playhouse to be able to do so. Even describing a typical Elizabethan playhouse is hazardous enough in view of the gaps in our knowledge and the differences which undoubtedly existed between actual examples. The attempt must be made, however, if *Doctor Faustus* is to be imagined in anything like the theatrical setting for which it was designed. A full account would necessarily be somewhat inconclusive on the numerous points on which scholars disagree; many of its statements would have to be highly qualified. What follows is a short account, with as few 'ifs' and 'buts', and as great a clarity and definiteness, as seems permissible.

1. The building

In Marlowe's England, the theatre had its enemies. The most vocal of these were the Puritans, so called from their conviction that the Protestant reformation of the church under Queen Elizabeth I had not gone far enough and that a further purification from Catholic forms and ceremonies was essential. Strict, precise, and scrupulous, they distrusted worldly pleasures; they abhorred the May-games and other traditional festivities: and they abominated stage-plays. Was not the wearing of women's clothes by the boys who took the female parts a flagrant defiance of Holy Scripture? Had not the Fathers of the church and even the worthier pagans condemned common players? Had not the pagan plays originated in idolatry? And who could deny that acting itself was a form of falsehood? Above all, Puritan propagandists insisted that the English drama of their time was blasphemous and immoral. Plays were the snares of the Devil; the theatre was 'the school of bawdry' and 'the chapel of Satan'; the playhouses were hotbeds of sexual vice.

Puritanism was strong in the middle class from which came the Lord Mayor and Corporation of the city of London. These men objected to the theatre not only as Puritans but also as civic dignitaries. Could it not tempt apprentices to rowdiness and idleness? Was it not responsible, in a city in which the plague was endemic, for much spreading of infection? Did it not provide a convenient rendezvous for criminal and turbulent characters? The case for suppressing it seemed strong.

The hostility of the civic authorities caused the builders of the first permanent playhouses in the London area, which were also the first in England, to choose sites just outside the jurisdiction of the city. Thus, the Theatre, the earliest of all, was erected slightly north of London in 1576. It was pulled down twenty-two years later, and the timber was used for building the Globe. This stood on the Bankside, to the south of the Thames, again just beyond the control of the Corporation. For a short time, London's entertainment industry flourished there. But throughout Marlowe's adult life the main centre of theatrical activity remained to the north of the city. In 1589, when he was involved in a sword-fight in Hog Lane, near Finsbury Fields, in the course of which his friend Thomas Watson, the poet, killed a man, Marlowe seems to have been living conveniently near to the playhouses in that area called the Theatre and the Curtain.

A typical public or open-air playhouse appears to have been a roughly cylindrical structure enclosing an unroofed circular yard. The yard was quite small. Its area was not much greater than that of a modern lawn-tennis court. Moreover, a good third of it was covered by a broad rectangular platform stage, about five feet high, which projected half-way across it in such a fashion as to leave space for the spectators on three sides. These spectators, generally known as the groundlings, had paid one penny for admission. They remained standing.

Members of the audience who were willing to pay an extra penny or twopence had access to the galleries, usually three in number, running round the inside wall of the building. Here they could sit under the shelter of a thatched or tiled roof. A seat in a 'private room' or box immediately adjoining the stage, or a stool on the stage itself, would cost sixpence or a shilling. The significance of these figures will be clear if we remember that sixpence was the price of a printed playbook or a good plain dinner.

The main part of the stage itself was the platform or apron-stage already described as projecting deeply into the yard. The wall at its rear was pierced by a wide central aperture admitting to a shallow discovery-space; this aperture could be closed by curtains. The section of the second gallery which ran immediately above the discovery-space seems normally to have been reserved for use by the players as a balcony or upper stage. This, too, could apparently be curtained off. From their own quarters, the tiring-house, which lay behind all these, the actors had access to the main stage through two doors flanking the central aperture in its rear wall; they had also direct access to the discovery-space and the upper stage.

Three secondary features of the physical structure have a special interest for students of *Doctor Faustus*. First, above each of the doors admitting the performers to the main stage, that is, on either side of the balcony or upper stage, there appears to have been a window. Second, the main stage was equipped with trap-doors for spectacular effects. Third, the main stage was covered over by a roof, known as the 'shadow' or 'heavens'. This sheltered the players from rain. Built partly over it and partly at the top of the tiring-house was a hut with machines and traps for aerial ascents and descents and, in particular, for the raising and lowering of the theatre's throne or 'state'. Discussion of the use made in *Doctor Faustus* of these facilities will be found in the notes on xi, 22; xii, 70, 83–9; xix, 105, 115, 132, 190.

No scenery was used in this theatre, except perhaps for an occasional backcloth in the discovery-space. A reference in the dialogue would suffice to suggest a particular locality when necessary: thus, the last line of the Prologue to *Doctor Faustus* tells us that Faustus in scene i is 'in his study'; and the opening lines of scene xi make it clear that the action has moved to the court of the Emperor Charles V. But very often the stage stood for 'nowhere in particular' or, to be more exact, 'any place where the characters on it may plausibly be supposed to have met'. This being so, an Elizabethan dramatist did not think himself obliged to state the locality at the head of each scene of his text. Modern editors have commonly done this for him; but it has seemed better in the present edition to follow the Elizabethan example. It does, after all, correspond more closely with what happened in the theatre.

On the bare main stage, in the middle of the tiny auditorium, almost the whole of each play would be presented. But the discovery-space and the upper stage – and possibly even parts of the yard, as suggested in the notes on xviii, 27, 98 – were also available. The players made suggestive use of these.

The discovery-space could stand for any narrowly confined area. When its curtains were drawn back at the beginning of scene i of *Doctor Faustus*, the protagonist was discovered there 'in his study'.

This does not mean that the space was as large as we should normally expect a study to be. It was probably just large enough for Faustus to sit in it with a few books on a small table. As he spoke his opening soliloquy, he would rise to his feet and advance to a more commanding position on the main stage. The whole main stage would then stand for the study which the discovery-space had initially suggested. In Shakespeare's theatre, the discovery-space would hold Portia's caskets in *The Merchant of Venice*, the supposed statue of Hermione in *The Winter's Tale*, and, no doubt filling it almost to capacity, the bed on which Juliet lies in a death-like trance in *Romeo and Juliet*.

The upper stage frequently served as the wall of a besieged city. In 1 *Henry VI*, it represented at different times the defences of no fewer than four. The text requires the actors to make bold and spectacular use of it; the defenders of one of the four cities have to leap from the wall 'in their shirts'. This stage-direction serves to remind us how small the Elizabethan theatre was. If actors could leap down from the upper to the main stage without injuring themselves, the difference in height can hardly have been much more than six feet. The upper stage served also as Juliet's balcony. When Henry VIII stood there to eavesdrop on his council, he was using it in a way that is of some interest to students of Marlowe's theatre. On a small stage, it can be very difficult to present a scene in which an eavesdropper has to be invisible to the other characters but in full view of the audience. Elizabethan producers got round this difficulty by allowing the eavesdropper to make a purely conventional use of the upper stage. We may reasonably suppose that it was so used by the diabolical characters who watch Faustus conjure in scene iii and who gloat over his agony in scene xix.

But an interest in these suggestive uses of the discovery-space and the upper stage must not be allowed to distract us from the central fact that nearly the whole of any play would be acted on the main stage in the middle of the small arena.

2. *The persons*

Who did this acting ? And who paid to see it ? A theatre is not only a building; it is also a company of players and an audience. The players call for our attention first.

Puritan enemies of the stage often taunted them with being vaga-
bonds and masterless men and, as such, liable to penalties under
the Poor Law of that time. No doubt they would have been over-
joyed to have seen them whipped accordingly at the cart-tail and
put to some honest labour. But their hopes were frustrated. Each
company enrolled itself among the servants of an obliging noble-
man or royal personage; and this nominal relationship, giving the
masterless men a nominal master, safeguarded the actors against
prosecution by Puritan office-bearers. Occasionally, of course, the
relationship might become more than merely nominal: the noble-
man might intervene to extricate his servants from a difficulty;
and he would naturally call upon them if he wished to provide a
private dramatic entertainment for his friends. But the players
drew no regular wage from him. They lived on what they earned
as players.

Marlowe wrote for the Lord Admiral's men, Shakespeare for the
Lord Chamberlain's men. After the accession of King James I in
1603, these groups came under royal protection as Prince Henry's
men and the King's men respectively. A member of such a company might pursue a steady and profitable career as an actor. Starting perhaps as an apprentice playing female parts – for there were no
actresses in the Elizabethan theatre – he might eventually become
a sharer, that is, one of the ten to fifteen senior members who shared
the box-office receipts after the rent, the wages of the hired actors,
and the other expenses had been paid.

On the stage, the actors wore costumes that were often very
splendid and always basically contemporary in style. If the play
were set in a remote time or a distant place, they might introduce symbolic items into their attire – a turban, for example, or a
Roman helmet. But these would not affect its essential contem-
poraneity.

A similar disregard for painstaking realism seems to have characterized the acting. This was rhetorical. In other words, the per-
former aimed less at the naturalistic impersonation of the character
whom the dramatist had apparently imagined than at the expressive
delivery, by flexibly controlled movement, attitude, and voice, of
the words which the dramatist had actually written. Mounted on a
high stage in a tiny arena, delivering his lines with formal elocution

and heightened gesture, and in his soliloquies and many of his set speeches directly addressing the audience itself, the actor had the opportunity of making every word tell. He could hardly have hoped for better material than the great monologues in *Doctor Faustus*. Opera provides the best modern parallel. In opera, impersonation, while important, is subordinate to singing; in the Elizabethan theatre, impersonation, while important, was subordinate to elocution.

At the same time, we must not underrate the appeal to the eye. Gestures were emphatic, movement was bold. Processions were stately, banquets lavish, battles bloody.

The leading player of the Admiral's men was Edward Alleyn. Born in 1566, he is said to have been 'bred a stage-player' and was certainly one by 1583. He married the step-daughter of Philip Henslowe, the theatre-manager, in 1592, and until Henslowe's death in 1616 the two men worked very successfully in partnership. Shortly after his first wife's death in 1623, Alleyn married the daughter of John Donne, the poet and Dean of St Paul's. He died in 1626.

During his later years he built and endowed Dulwich College; but as a young man he put his energies mainly into acting. He played Tamburlaine, Barabas, and Faustus; there is contemporary testimony to the beauty of his voice; he is believed to have excelled as a tyrant, and he certainly gave an extraordinary vogue to Tamburlaine's line, 'Holla, ye pampered jades of Asia!'

He and his fellows, like their colleagues in other companies, operated a kind of repertory system. At any one time, they had a considerable number of plays rehearsed and ready for performance. Normally, they acted a different play on each afternoon of the week, but they repeated plays fairly frequently. A work of average popularity would be put on about once weekly for approximately a dozen weeks. It would then be dropped, and a new piece might be adopted instead of it. Old plays of great popularity were often revived – occasionally, after revision – at later dates. *Doctor Faustus* was revised in 1602, when Henslowe paid two writers £4 for making additions to it which are believed to have perished. It was revised again sixty years later, when, perhaps in view of the theological complexion of the newly restored Stuart dynasty, a scene at the court of the Soldan in Babylon replaced the scenes at the papal court.

What was the composition of the theatregoing public? The Puritans claimed to know.

> Now the common haunters [of playhouses] are for the most part the lewdest persons in the land, apt for pilfery, perjury, forgery, or any rogueries, the very scum, rascality, and baggage of the people, thieves, cutpurses, shifters, cozeners; briefly, an unclean generation and spawn of vipers. Must not here be good rule, where is such a brood of Hell-bred creatures? For a play is like a sink in a town, whereunto all the filth doth run; or a boil in the body, that draweth all the ill humours unto it.

We may legitimately doubt the testimony of a witness who so passionately enjoys testifying. What is more, Puritan witnesses described the drama itself in much the same terms, and in this case the survival of the texts has enabled us to detect their misrepresentations. Is it not on the face of it likely that they were equally guilty of distortion when they described the audiences?

Recent research has demonstrated their unreliability. The theatres in which the better companies played – and the Admiral's men as well as the Chamberlain's men must be counted among these – attracted a fairly representative cross-section of the London population. Of course, members of some social groups found it easier to spare the time and money for playgoing than did others; but all important groups seem to have been represented, apart from the very young, the very old, and, naturally, the Puritans. Men outnumbered women, but plenty of respectable women attended – often in family theatre-parties. Disreputable characters – pickpockets, for example, and prostitutes – were undeniably present, but they were too few to deter decent visitors. The atmosphere was not sinister but gay.

These people were eager and attentive listeners. At a time when illiteracy was widespread, talking inevitably occupied much of the place in daily life now occupied by reading. In consequence, men and women were highly trained in listening to the spoken language and in responding to it. Moreover, the Elizabethans were less inhibited in expressing their responses than are modern playgoers. They laughed mightily; they wept unashamedly; they hissed and mewed at what they disliked; and they clapped and cheered at what pleased them. They could be noisy while waiting for a show to start; but at two o'clock, when the well-known actors advanced almost to the centre of the tiny arena and the play began to live, they became orderly and attentive enough.

10. STAGE-HISTORY OF *Doctor Faustus*

Just as we cannot be certain when *Doctor Faustus* was written, so we cannot say which company first performed it. What we do know is that in 1594, when it was no longer a new play, Edward Alleyn and the Admiral's men were acting it with great success at the Bankside theatre called the Rose. It remained in demand throughout the 1590's, and the indications are that it never completely lost its popularity before the closing of the theatres by the Puritans on the outbreak of the Civil War in 1642. At all events, Prince Charles' men were playing it at the Fortune theatre a year or so prior to that event. It was even exported: a touring company of English actors took it to Austria in 1608.

An account published in 1620 sheds light on current methods of production. At the Fortune theatre, we learn, where the company formerly known as Prince Henry's men and now called the Palsgrave's men was presenting Marlowe's play, 'a man may behold shag-haired devils run roaring over the stage with squibs in their mouths, while drummers make thunder in the tiring-house and the twelvepenny hirelings make artificial lightning in their heavens.' Horrified by such goings-on, the Puritans circulated cautionary tales. One of these concerns the visible appearance of the Devil himself upon the stage while *Doctor Faustus* was being played at the Belsavage theatre during Queen Elizabeth's reign 'to the great amazement both of the actors and spectators . . . , there being some distracted [i.e., driven mad] with that fearful sight'. According to another, some touring players at Exeter were overwhelmed in the course of a performance of *Doctor Faustus* by the dreadful certainty that 'there was one devil too many amongst them'. Detecting their fear, the audience panicked. The actors, 'contrary to their custom', spent the night 'in reading and in prayer'.

Closed in 1642, the theatres reopened on the restoration of the monarchy in 1660. *Doctor Faustus* returned to the stage in a slightly revised form. Samuel Pepys and his wife saw it, 'wretchedly and poorly done' in 1662; and it was performed before royalty in 1675. It then disappeared from the English theatre for two centuries.

Faustus himself did not disappear. Until the end of the eighteenth century, he continued to entertain the populace in farces, pantomimes, and puppet-plays. But during all this time Marlowe's serious treatment of the legend was neither acted nor even printed. No doubt the story seemed absurd to polite and sceptical eighteenth-century intelligences.

In the Romantic period, naturally enough, interest began to revive. *Doctor Faustus* came back into print in 1814, and further editions followed regularly and quite frequently. For a long time, however, various operatic and other more or less free adaptations of Goethe's *Faust* met what demand there was to have the legend staged. At last, in 1896, Marlowe's tragedy received its first performance since 1675.

Since then, it has often been presented in England and elsewhere. Orson Welles' production of 1937, which ran for six months in New York, is now generally regarded as one of the landmarks of the twentieth-century American theatre. Following it, there have been three Old Vic productions – the last of them opening at the Edinburgh Festival of 1961 – and the play has twice appeared in the programme of the Shakespeare Memorial Theatre, Stratford. Provincial and touring companies and amateur dramatic societies have revived it. The B.B.C. has broadcast more than a dozen productions of it, either on sound radio or on television. *Doctor Faustus* is today, in fact, one of the most frequently performed of plays by contemporaries of Shakespeare.

Orson Welles' production of 1937 was only his first sponsoring of Faustus. In Paris in 1950 he presented *Time Runs*, his own version of the story, based on the relevant works of Marlowe, Milton, and Dante. Eartha Kitt acted Helen to Welles' Faustus, and Duke Ellington provided the music.

II. TEXT OF *Doctor Faustus*

The text of *Doctor Faustus* printed in the present edition differs considerably from the text of the play given in some other editions. This fact calls for explanation.

All modern texts of *Doctor Faustus* derive directly or indirectly from one or both of two early versions: the so-called A-version, first published in 1604, and the so-called B-version, first published in 1616. Of these, the B-version is longer than the A-version by more than one-third. The A-version knows nothing of Bruno the antipope either at the papal or at the imperial court; it knows nothing of the plan of revenge by Benvolio and his friends or of its frustration by Faustus; it is equally ignorant of the conspiracy of the Horse-courser and his associates and of their humiliation at Vanholt; and it omits from the last three scenes a number of incidents, mainly of a supernatural or spectacular kind. In addition, all scenes occurring in both versions differ appreciably in wording, and five of them differ very widely indeed.

For a long time, editors of *Doctor Faustus* supposed that, since the longer B-version was published later than the shorter A-version, B must represent a revision and expansion of A. But in 1950 the great bibliographer W. W. Greg demonstrated that B, although not printed until twelve years after A, must already have been in existence when A was composed; and that A represents an abbreviated reconstruction of it from memory by a group of players who wished to acquire a text of the play for performance.

Until 1950, most editors had based their texts upon the shorter version, believing that this was the more original. Greg's demonstration that the longer version is the more original has caused editors to rely instead upon B. But they cannot rely upon it completely. When it was first printed in 1616, certain passages in the manuscript must have been illegible, for the compositor, or the scribe who prepared his copy for him, helped himself out with a printed copy of A. Clearly, in places where B is merely following A, and not succeeding in following it exactly, A itself is preferable to B. Nor are these the only circumstances in which an editor, while relying mainly upon B, will make use of A. But it would be inappropriate to repeat here the whole of an analysis which Greg states in detail in his parallel-text edition of *Doctor Faustus*, and which the present editor describes fairly fully and criticizes in minor respects in the introduction to his 'Revels' edition of the play. All that is immediately important is that the text of *Doctor Faustus* printed in the present edition is based mainly, but not exclusively, upon the version first published in 1616; that the reasons dictating this editorial policy are marshalled by Greg and reviewed in the 'Revels' edition of the play; and that modern scholarship encourages us to believe that a text such as is given here is closer to what Marlowe and another wrote than is the short version which is all that many readers used to know.

One typographical feature of the present edition may be mentioned finally. Certain stage-directions and portions of stage-directions are printed in square brackets. These words and phrases are editorial additions. All stage-directions and portions of stage-directions not enclosed in this way derive from the editions of 1616 and 1604.

THE TRAGICAL HISTORY OF
THE LIFE AND DEATH OF
DOCTOR FAUSTUS

Dramatis Personae

CHORUS.

DOCTOR JOHN FAUSTUS.

WAGNER, *a student, his servant.*

VALDES,
CORNELIUS, } *friends to Faustus.*

THREE SCHOLARS, *students under Faustus*

AN OLD MAN.

POPE ADRIAN.

RAYMOND, *King of Hungary.*

BRUNO, *the rival Pope.*   10

THE CARDINALS OF FRANCE AND PADUA.

THE ARCHBISHOP OF RHEIMS.

CHARLES V, *Emperor of Germany.*

MARTINO,
FREDERICK, } *gentlemen at his court.*
BENVOLIO,

THE DUKE OF SAXONY.

THE DUKE OF VANHOLT.

THE DUCHESS OF VANHOLT.

BISHOPS, MONKS, FRIARS, SOLDIERS, *and* ATTENDANTS.   20

ROBIN, *called the Clown.*

DICK.

A VINTNER.

A HORSE-COURSER.

A CARTER.

A HOSTESS.

GOOD ANGEL.

BAD ANGEL.

MEPHOSTOPHILIS.

23. *Vintner:* innkeeper selling wine.
24. *Horse-courser:* horse-dealer.

NOTES: p. 149

LUCIFER.   30
BEELZEBUB.
PRIDE,
COVETOUSNESS,
ENVY,
WRATH,   } the Seven Deadly Sins.
GLUTTONY,
SLOTH,
LECHERY,
ALEXANDER THE GREAT,
HIS PARAMOUR,   40
DARIUS, *King of Persia,*   } spirits.
HELEN,
TWO CUPIDS,
DEVILS *and* A PIPER.

40. *Paramour:* mistress.

NOTES: p. 149

Prologue

Enter Chorus.

CHO. Not marching in the fields of Trasimene
Where Mars did mate the warlike Carthagens,
Nor sporting in the dalliance of love
In courts of kings where state is overturn'd,
Nor in the pomp of proud audacious deeds
Intends our muse to vaunt his heavenly verse:
Only this, gentles – we must now perform
The form of Faustus' fortunes, good or bad:
And now to patient judgements we appeal,
And speak for Faustus in his infancy.   10
Now is he born, of parents base of stock,
In Germany, within a town call'd Rhode;
At riper years to Wittenberg he went,
Whereas his kinsmen chiefly brought him up.
So much he profits in divinity,
The fruitful plot of scholarism grac'd,
That shortly he was grac'd with doctor's name,
Excelling all, and sweetly can dispute
In th' heavenly matters of theology;
Till, swollen with cunning of a self-conceit,   20
His waxen wings did mount above his reach,
And, melting, heavens conspir'd his overthrow;
For, falling to a devilish exercise,
And glutted now with learning's golden gifts,

2. *mate:* ally himself with.
4. *state:* government.
6. *our muse:* our poet.
vaunt: display proudly.
7. *gentles:* gentlefolk.
14. *Whereas:* where.
15. *profits:* makes progress.
18. *sweetly:* persuasively.

NOTES: p. 150

He surfeits upon cursed necromancy;
Nothing so sweet as magic is to him,
Which he prefers before his chiefest bliss:
And this the man that in his study sits.　　　　　*Exit.*

25. *necromancy:* black magic (literally, divination by means of the dead).

NOTES : p. 150

Soliloquy – An internal monologue.
Means no other characters are on stage.

Scene I

FAUSTUS *in his study.*

FAU. Settle thy studies, Faustus, and begin
　　To sound the depth of that thou wilt profess;
　　Having commenc'd, be a divine in show,
　　Yet level at the end of every art,
　　And live and die in Aristotle's works.
　　Sweet Analytics, 'tis thou hast ravish'd me!
　　Bene disserere est finis logices.
　　Is to dispute well logic's chiefest end?
　　Affords this art no greater miracle?
　　Then read no more, thou hast attain'd that end;　　10
　　A greater subject fitteth Faustus' wit.
　　Bid *on kai me on* farewell, Galen come,
　　Seeing *ubi desinit philosophus, ibi incipit medicus.*
　　Be a physician, Faustus, heap up gold,
　　And be eterniz'd for some wondrous cure.
　　Summum bonum medicinae sanitas,
　　The end of physic is our body's health.
　　Why, Faustus, hast thou not attain'd that end?
　　Is not thy common talk sound aphorisms?
　　Are not thy bills hung up as monuments,　　20
　　Whereby whole cities have escap'd the plague
　　And thousand desperate maladies been cur'd?
　　Yet art thou still but Faustus, and a man.

  1. *Settle:* make a definite choice of.
  2. *profess:* claim proficiency in and teach.
  3. *commenc'd:* graduated.
  4. *level:* aim.
  8. *dispute:* carry on a disputation.
  11. *wit:* understanding.
  15. *eterniz'd:* made eternally famous.
  19. *sound aphorisms:* reliable medical precepts.
  20. *bills:* prescriptions.
  22. *maladies:* individual cases of sickness.

NOTES: pp. 150–1

Couldst thou make men to live eternally
Or being dead raise them to life again,
Then this profession were to be esteem'd.
Physic, farewell! Where is Justinian?
Si una eademque res legatur duobus, alter rem, alter valorem
rei, etc.
A petty case of paltry legacies!   30
Exhereditare filium non potest pater, nisi –
Such is the subject of the Institute
And universal body of the law.
This study fits a mercenary drudge
Who aims at nothing but external trash,
Too servile and illiberal for me.
When all is done, divinity is best.
Jerome's Bible, Faustus, view it well.
Stipendium peccati mors est. Ha! *Stipendium, etc.* The
reward of sin is death: that's hard. *Si peccasse negamus,*   40
fallimur, et nulla est in nobis veritas. If we say that we
have no sin, we deceive ourselves, and there's no truth in
us. Why, then, belike we must sin, and so consequently
die.
Ay, we must die an everlasting death.
What doctrine call you this? *Che sarà, sarà:*
What will be, shall be! Divinity, adieu!
These metaphysics of magicians
And necromantic books are heavenly;
Lines, circles, letters, and characters: 50
Ay, these are those that Faustus most desires.
O, what a world of profit and delight,
Of power, of honour, of omnipotence,
Is promis'd to the studious artisan!
All things that move between the quiet poles
Shall be at my command: emperors and kings

35. *trash:* money (a contemptuous term).
37. *When all is done:* after all.
48. *metaphysics:* supernatural arts.
54. *artisan:* artist.

Are but obey'd in their several provinces,
Nor can they raise the wind or rend the clouds;
But his dominion that exceeds in this
Stretcheth as far as doth the mind of man: 60
A sound magician is a demi-god;
Here tire, my brains, to get a deity!

Enter WAGNER.

Wagner, commend me to my dearest friends,
The German Valdes and Cornelius;
Request them earnestly to visit me.
WAG. I will, sir.   *Exit.*
FAU. Their conference will be a greater help to me
Than all my labours, plod I ne'er so fast.

Enter the Angel *and* Spirit.

GOOD ANG. O Faustus, lay that damned book aside
And gaze not on it lest it tempt thy soul   70
And heap God's heavy wrath upon thy head.
Read, read the scriptures; that is blasphemy.
BAD ANG. Go forward, Faustus, in that famous art
Wherein all nature's treasury is contain'd:
Be thou on earth as Jove is in the sky,
Lord and commander of these elements.   *Exeunt* Angels.
FAU. How am I glutted with conceit of this!
Shall I make spirits fetch me what I please,
Resolve me of all ambiguities,
Perform what desperate enterprise I will?   80
I'll have them fly to India for gold,
Ransack the ocean for orient pearl,

57. *several:* respective.
62. *tire:* exhaust yourselves.   *get:* beget.
67. *conference:* conversation.
76. *these elements:* the elements (earth, water, air, and fire).
77. *conceit:* thought.
79. *Resolve me of:* free me from doubt concerning.
80. *desperate:* impossibly difficult.
82. *orient:* lustrous (strictly, from the eastern seas).

NOTES: p. 152

And search all corners of the new-found world
For pleasant fruits and princely delicates;
I'll have them read me strange philosophy
And tell the secrets of all foreign kings;
I'll have them wall all Germany with brass
And make swift Rhine circle fair Wittenberg;
I'll have them fill the public schools with silk
Wherewith the students shall be bravely clad;   90
I'll levy soldiers with the coin they bring
And chase the Prince of Parma from our land
And reign sole king of all our provinces;
Yea, stranger engines for the brunt of war
Than was the fiery keel at Antwerp's bridge
I'll make my servile spirits to invent.

Enter VALDES *and* CORNELIUS.

Come, German Valdes and Cornelius,
And make me blest with your sage conference.
Valdes, sweet Valdes, and Cornelius,
Know that your words have won me at the last   100
To practise magic and concealed arts;
Yet not your words only, but mine own fantasy,
That will receive no object, for my head
But ruminates on necromantic skill.
Philosophy is odious and obscure,
Both law and physic are for petty wits,
Divinity is basest of the three,
Unpleasant, harsh, contemptible, and vile;

84. *delicates:* delicacies.
88. *circle:* encircle.
89. *the public schools:* the university lecture-rooms.
90. *bravely:* splendidly.
94. *engines:* mechanical contrivances.
brunt: assault, onset.
98. *conference:* conversation.
102. *fantasy:* imagination.
104. *But:* only.
106. *wits:* minds.

NOTES: p. 153

'Tis magic, magic, that hath ravish'd me.
Then, gentle friends, aid me in this attempt,   110
And I, that have with concise syllogisms
Gravell'd the pastors of the German church,
And made the flowering pride of Wittenberg
Swarm to my problems as the infernal spirits
On sweet Musaeus when he came to hell,
Will be as cunning as Agrippa was,
Whose shadows made all Europe honour him.

VAL. Faustus, these books, thy wit, and our experience
Shall make all nations to canonize us.
As Indian Moors obey their Spanish lords,   120
So shall the spirits of every element
Be always serviceable to us three:
Like lions shall they guard us when we please,
Like Almain rutters with their horsemen's staves
Or Lapland giants trotting by our sides;
Sometimes like women or unwedded maids,
Shadowing more beauty in their airy brows
Than in the white breasts of the queen of love.
From Venice shall they drag huge argosies,
And from America the golden fleece   130
That yearly stuffs old Philip's treasury,
If learned Faustus will be resolute.

FAU. Valdes, as resolute am I in this
As thou to live; therefore object it not.

CORN. The miracles that magic will perform
Will make thee vow to study nothing else.
He that is grounded in astrology,

111. *syllogisms:* logically binding arguments.
112. *Gravell'd:* brought to a stop, nonplussed.
113. *flowering pride:* best students.
114. *problems:* questions proposed for scholastic disputation.
116. *cunning:* skilful.
118. *wit:* understanding.
127. *Shadowing:* harbouring.
airy: ethereal, heavenly.
129. *argosies:* large merchant-vessels.

NOTES: pp. 153-4

Enrich'd with tongues, well seen in minerals,
Hath all the principles magic doth require;
Then doubt not, Faustus, but to be renown'd   140
And more frequented for this mystery
Than heretofore the Delphian oracle.
The spirits tell me they can dry the sea
And fetch the treasure of all foreign wrecks,
Ay, all the wealth that our forefathers hid
Within the massy entrails of the earth.
Then tell me, Faustus, what shall we three want?

FAU. Nothing, Cornelius. O, this cheers my soul!
Come, show me some demonstrations magical,
That I may conjure in some lusty grove   150
And have these joys in full possession.

VAL. Then haste thee to some solitary grove,
And bear wise Bacon's and Abanus' works,
The Hebrew Psalter, and New Testament;
And whatsoever else is requisite
We will inform thee ere our conference cease.

CORN. Valdes, first let him know the words of art,
And then, all other ceremonies learn'd,
Faustus may try his cunning by himself.

VAL. First I'll instruct thee in the rudiments,   160
And then wilt thou be perfecter than I.

FAU. Then come and dine with me, and after meat
We'll canvass every quiddity thereof,
For ere I sleep I'll try what I can do:
This night I'll conjure though I die therefor.   *Exeunt omnes.*

139. *principles:* rudiments.
141. *frequented:* resorted to.   *mystery:* skill, art.
146. *massy:* massive.
150. *conjure:* call up spirits.   *lusty:* pleasant.
159. *cunning:* skill.
163. *canvass:* discuss.
quiddity: essential part (a scholastic term).
165. *therefor:* for it.
Stage-direction: *omnes:* all.

NOTES: pp. 154–5

Scene II

Enter two Scholars.

1 SCH. I wonder what's become of Faustus, that was wont to make our schools ring with *sic probo*.

Enter WAGNER.

2 SCH. That shall we presently know; here comes his boy.

1 SCH. How now, sirrah, where's thy master?

WAG. God in heaven knows.

2 SCH. Why, dost not thou know then?

WAG. Yes, I know; but that follows not.

1 SCH. Go to, sirrah, leave your jesting and tell us where he is.

WAG. That follows not by force of argument, which you, being licentiates, should stand upon; therefore acknowledge   10 your error and be attentive.

2 SCH. Then you will not tell us?

WAG. You are deceived, for I will tell you. Yet, if you were not dunces, you would never ask me such a question. For is he not *corpus naturale*? and is not that *mobile*? Then wherefore should you ask me such a question? But that I am by nature phlegmatic, slow to wrath, and prone to lechery (to love, I would say), it were not for you to come within forty foot of the place of execution – although I do not doubt but to see you both hanged the next sessions. Thus having   20 triumphed over you, I will set my countenance like a precisian and begin to speak thus: Truly, my dear brethren, my master is within at dinner with Valdes and Cornelius, as this wine, if it could speak, would inform your worships: and so the Lord bless you, preserve you, and keep you, my dear brethren.   *Exit.*

3. *presently:* directly, at once.
boy: servant.
8. *Go to:* come, come!
10. *stand:* rely.
15–16. *wherefore:* to what end.
21–2. *precisian:* Puritan.

NOTES: p. 155

1 SCH. O Faustus, then I fear that which I have long suspected,
      That thou art fallen into that damned art
      For which they two are infamous through the world.
2 SCH. Were he a stranger, not ally'd to me,   30
      The danger of his soul would make me mourn.
      But come, let us go and inform the Rector:
      It may be his grave counsel may reclaim him.
1 SCH. I fear me, nothing will reclaim him now.
2 SCH. Yet let us see what we can do.   *Exeunt.*

Scene III

Thunder. Enter LUCIFER *and four* Devils [*above*]:
FAUSTUS *to them with this speech.*

FAU. Now that the gloomy shadow of the night,
      Longing to view Orion's drizzling look,
      Leaps from th' antarctic world unto the sky
      And dims the welkin with her pitchy breath,
      Faustus, begin thine incantations,
      And try if devils will obey thy hest,
      Seeing thou hast pray'd and sacrific'd to them.
      Within this circle is Jehovah's name
      Forward and backward anagrammatiz'd,
      The breviated names of holy saints,   10
      Figures of every adjunct to the heavens,
      And characters of signs and erring stars,
      By which the spirits are enforc'd to rise:
      Then fear not, Faustus, to be resolute
      And try the uttermost magic can perform.   *Thunder.*
      Sint mihi dei Acherontis propitii! Valeat numen triplex
      Iehovae! Ignei, aerii, aquatici, terreni spiritus salvete!

32. *Rector:* head of the university.
4. *welkin:* sky.
6. *hest:* command.
10. *breviated:* abbreviated.
11. *adjunct to:* heavenly body fixed to, or suspended in.

NOTES: pp. 155-6

Orientis princeps Lucifer, Beelzebub inferni ardentis mon-
archa, et Demogorgon, propitiamus vos ut appareat et surgat
Mephostophilis!   20

           Dragon [*appears briefly above*].

Quid tu moraris? Per Iehovam, Gehennam, et consecratam
aquam quam nunc spargo, signumque crucis quod nunc facio,
et per vota nostra, ipse nunc surgat nobis dicatus Mephosto-
philis!

           Enter a Devil.

I charge thee to return and change thy shape;
Thou art too ugly to attend on me.
Go, and return an old Franciscan friar,
That holy shape becomes a devil best.   *Exit* Devil.
I see there's virtue in my heavenly words.
Who would not be proficient in this art?   30
How pliant is this Mephostophilis,
Full of obedience and humility!
Such is the force of magic and my spells.
Now, Faustus, thou art conjuror laureate,
That canst command great Mephostophilis.
Quin redis, Mephostophilis, fratris imagine!

           Enter MEPHOSTOPHILIS.

MEPH. Now, Faustus, what wouldst thou have me do?
FAU. I charge thee wait upon me whilst I live,
    To do whatever Faustus shall command,
    Be it to make the moon drop from her sphere   40
    Or the ocean to overwhelm the world.
MEPH. I am a servant to great Lucifer
    And may not follow thee without his leave;
    No more than he commands must we perform.

---

29. *virtue:* power.
heavenly words: scriptural phrases used for conjuration.
34. *conjuror laureate:* a conjuror worthy of special distinction.

NOTES: p. 156

FAU. Did not he charge thee to appear to me?

MEPH. No, I came hither of mine own accord.

FAU. Did not my conjuring speeches raise thee? Speak.

MEPH. That was the cause, but yet *per accidens*:
    For when we hear one rack the name of God,
    Abjure the scriptures and his saviour Christ,   50
    We fly, in hope to get his glorious soul;
    Nor will we come unless he use such means
    Whereby he is in danger to be damn'd.
    Therefore the shortest cut for conjuring
    Is stoutly to abjure the Trinity
    And pray devoutly to the prince of hell.

FAU. So Faustus hath
    Already done, and holds this principle,
    There is no chief but only Beelzebub,
    To whom Faustus doth dedicate himself.   60
    This word 'damnation' terrifies not him,
    For he confounds hell in Elysium:
    His ghost be with the old philosophers!
    But, leaving these vain trifles of men's souls,
    Tell me, what is that Lucifer thy lord?

MEPH. Arch-regent and commander of all spirits.

FAU. Was not that Lucifer an angel once?

MEPH. Yes, Faustus, and most dearly lov'd of God.

FAU. How comes it then that he is prince of devils?

MEPH. O, by aspiring pride and insolence,   70
    For which God threw him from the face of heaven.

FAU. And what are you that live with Lucifer?

MEPH. Unhappy spirits that fell with Lucifer,
    Conspir'd against our God with Lucifer,
    And are for ever damn'd with Lucifer.

FAU. Where are you damn'd?

MEPH.   In hell.

---

49. *rack:* torment by anagrammatizing.

51. *glorious:* splendid in beauty (with perhaps some suggestion of 'boastful, presumptuous').

63. *ghost:* spirit.

NOTES: p. 157

FAU. How comes it then that thou art out of hell?
MEPH. Why, this is hell, nor am I out of it.
    Think'st thou that I, who saw the face of God
    And tasted the eternal joys of heaven,   80
    Am not tormented with ten thousand hells
    In being depriv'd of everlasting bliss?
    O Faustus, leave these frivolous demands,
    Which strike a terror to my fainting soul.
FAU. What, is great Mephostophilis so passionate
    For being deprived of the joys of heaven?
    Learn thou of Faustus manly fortitude
    And scorn those joys thou never shalt possess.
    Go bear these tidings to great Lucifer:
    Seeing Faustus hath incurr'd eternal death   90
    By desperate thoughts against Jove's deity,
    Say he surrenders up to him his soul
    So he will spare him four-and-twenty years,
    Letting him live in all voluptuousness,
    Having thee ever to attend on me,
    To give me whatsoever I shall ask,
    To tell me whatsoever I demand,
    To slay mine enemies and aid my friends,
    And always be obedient to my will.
    Go, and return to mighty Lucifer,   100
    And meet me in my study at midnight,
    And then resolve me of thy master's mind.
MEPH. I will, Faustus.   *Exit.*
FAU. Had I as many souls as there be stars,
    I'd give them all for Mephostophilis.
    By him I'll be great emperor of the world,
    And make a bridge thorough the moving air
    To pass the ocean with a band of men;

    83. *demands:* questions.
    85. *passionate:* stirred by strong feeling.
    93. *So:* on condition that.
    102. *resolve me of:* inform me concerning.
    107. *thorough:* through.

NOTES: p. 157

I'll join the hills that bind the Afric shore
And make that country continent to Spain,   110
And both contributory to my crown;
The Emperor shall not live but by my leave,
Nor any potentate of Germany.
Now that I have obtain'd what I desire,
I'll live in speculation of this art
Till Mephostophilis return again.   *Exit.*
                    [*Exeunt* LUCIFER *and* Devils.]

Scene IV

Enter WAGNER *and the* Clown [ROBIN].

WAG. Come hither, sirrah boy.

ROB. Boy! O, disgrace to my person! Zounds, boy in your face!
    You have seen many boys with such pickedevants, I am
    sure.

WAG. Sirrah, hast thou no comings in?

ROB. Yes, and goings out too, you may see, sir.

WAG. Alas, poor slave! see how poverty jests in his nakedness.
    I know the villain's out of service, and so hungry that I
    know he would give his soul to the devil for a shoulder of
    mutton, though it were blood-raw.   10

ROB. Not so, neither. I had need to have it well roasted, and
    good sauce to it, if I pay so dear, I can tell you.

WAG. Sirrah, wilt thou be my man and wait on me? and I will
    make thee go like *Qui mihi discipulus*.

ROB. What, in verse?

WAG. No, slave, in beaten silk and stavesacre.

109. *bind:* enclose.
110. *continent to:* continuous with.
111. *contributory:* subject.
115. *speculation:* contemplation, profound study.
2. *Zounds:* by God's wounds (an oath).
3. *pickedevants:* fashionable pointed beards.
8. *villain:* wretch.   *out of service:* unemployed.
16. *stavesacre:* the seeds of a kind of delphinium used to destroy
vermin.

ROB. Stavesacre! that's good to kill vermin. Then, belike, if I serve you, I shall be lousy.

WAG. Why, so thou shalt be, whether thou dost it or no; for, sirrah, if thou dost not presently bind thyself to me for   20
seven years, I'll turn all the lice about thee into familiars and make them tear thee in pieces.

ROB. Nay, sir, you may save yourself a labour, for they are as familiar with me as if they paid for their meat and drink, I can tell you.

WAG. Well, sirrah, leave your jesting and take these guilders.

ROB. Yes, marry, sir, and I thank you too.

WAG. So, now thou art to be at an hour's warning, whensoever and wheresoever the devil shall fetch thee.

ROB. Here, take your guilders again, I'll none of 'em.   30

WAG. Not I, thou art pressed, prepare thyself, for I will presently raise up two devils to carry thee away. Banio! Belcher!

ROB. Belcher! And Belcher come here, I'll belch him. I am not afraid of a devil.

Enter two Devils, *and the* Clown *runs up and down crying.*

WAG. How now, sir, will you serve me now?

ROB. Ay, good Wagner, take away the devil then.

WAG. Spirits, away!   *Exeunt* [Devils].
Now, sirrah, follow me.

ROB. I will, sir. But hark you, master, will you teach me this   40
conjuring occupation?

WAG. Ay, sirrah, I'll teach thee to turn thyself to a dog, or a cat, or a mouse, or a rat, or anything.

ROB. A dog, or a cat, or a mouse, or a rat! O brave, Wagner!

17. *belike:* probably.
20. *presently:* immediately.
21. *familiars:* attendant demons.
28. *warning:* notice.
30. *again:* back.
31. *pressed:* hired, engaged.
34. *And:* if.
44. *brave:* excellent, fine.

NOTES: p. 158

WAG. Villain, call me Master Wagner, and see that you walk
        attentively, and let your right eye be always diametrally
        fixed upon my left heel, that thou mayest *quasi vestigiis
        nostris insistere.*

ROB. Well, sir, I warrant you.   *Exeunt.*

Scene V

Enter FAUSTUS *in his study.*

FAU. Now, Faustus, must
        Thou needs be damn'd, and canst thou not be sav'd.
        What boots it then to think of God or heaven?
        Away with such vain fancies, and despair;
        Despair in God, and trust in Beelzebub.
        Now go not backward; no, Faustus, be resolute:
        Why waver'st thou? O, something soundeth in mine ears,
        'Abjure this magic, turn to God again!'
        Ay, and Faustus will turn to God again.
        To God? He loves thee not;   10
        The god thou serv'st is thine own appetite,
        Wherein is fix'd the love of Beelzebub:
        To him I'll build an altar and a church
        And offer lukewarm blood of new-born babes.

Enter the two Angels.

BAD ANG. Go forward, Faustus, in that famous art.
GOOD ANG. Sweet Faustus, leave that execrable art.
FAU. Contrition, prayer, repentance, what of these?
GOOD ANG. O, they are means to bring thee unto heaven.
BAD ANG. Rather illusions, fruits of lunacy,
        That make men foolish that do use them most.   20
GOOD ANG. Sweet Faustus, think of heaven and heavenly things.
BAD ANG. No, Faustus, think of honour and of wealth.

                                               Exeunt Angels.

FAU. Wealth!

                46. *diametrally:* directly, in a straight line.
                3. *boots:* avails.

                        NOTES: pp. 158-9

Why, the signory of Emden shall be mine.
When Mephostophilis shall stand by me,
What power can hurt me ? Faustus, thou art safe:
Cast no more doubts! Mephostophilis, come,
And bring glad tidings from great Lucifer.
Is't not midnight ? Come, Mephostophilis,
Veni, veni, Mephostophilis!   30

Enter MEPHOSTOPHILIS.

Now tell me what saith Lucifer thy lord ?
MEPH. That I shall wait on Faustus whilst he lives,
    So he will buy my service with his soul.
FAU. Already Faustus hath hazarded that for thee.
MEPH. But now thou must bequeath it solemnly
    And write a deed of gift with thine own blood,
    For that security craves Lucifer.
    If thou deny it, I must back to hell.
FAU. Stay, Mephostophilis, and tell me what good
    Will my soul do thy lord ?
MEPH.   Enlarge his kingdom.   40
FAU. Is that the reason why he tempts us thus ?
MEPH. *Solamen miseris socios habuisse doloris.*
FAU. Why, have you any pain that torture other ?
MEPH. As great as have the human souls of men.
    But tell me, Faustus, shall I have thy soul ?
    And I will be thy slave and wait on thee
    And give thee more than thou hast wit to ask.
FAU. Ay, Mephostophilis, I'll give it him.
MEPH. Then, Faustus, stab thy arm courageously,
    And bind thy soul, that at some certain day   50
    Great Lucifer may claim it as his own;

24. *signory:* lordship.
27. *Cast:* consider, ponder.
33. *So:* on condition that.
43. *other:* others.
47. *wit:* power of imagination.
50. *bind:* give a bond for.

NOTES: p. 159

And then be thou as great as Lucifer.

FAU. Lo, Mephostophilis, for love of thee
    Faustus hath cut his arm, and with his proper blood
    Assures his soul to be great Lucifer's,
    Chief lord and regent of perpetual night.
    View here this blood that trickles from mine arm,
    And let it be propitious for my wish.

MEPH. But, Faustus,
    Write it in manner of a deed of gift.   60

FAU. Ay, so I do. But, Mephostophilis,
    My blood congeals, and I can write no more.

MEPH. I'll fetch thee fire to dissolve it straight.   *Exit.*

FAU. What might the staying of my blood portend?
    Is it unwilling I should write this bill?
    Why streams it not, that I may write afresh?
    'Faustus gives to thee his soul': O, there it stay'd.
    Why shouldst thou not? is not thy soul thine own?
    Then write again: 'Faustus gives to thee his soul'.

Enter MEPHOSTOPHILIS *with the chafer of fire.*

MEPH. See, Faustus, here is fire; set it on.   70

FAU. So, now the blood begins to clear again:
    Now will I make an end immediately.

MEPH. [*Aside*] What will not I do to obtain his soul!

FAU. *Consummatum est*: this bill is ended,
    And Faustus hath bequeath'd his soul to Lucifer.
    But what is this inscription on mine arm?
    Homo fuge! Whither should I fly?
    If unto God, he'll throw me down to hell. –
    My senses are deceiv'd, here's nothing writ. –
    O yes, I see it plain; even here is writ,   80
    Homo fuge! Yet shall not Faustus fly.

54. *proper:* own.
55. *Assures:* conveys by deed.
64. *staying:* standing still.
65. *bill:* deed.
69. Stage-direction: *chafer:* portable grate.

NOTES: p. 159

MEPH. [*Aside*] I'll fetch him somewhat to delight his mind. *Exit.*

Enter Devils, *giving crowns and rich apparel*
to FAUSTUS. *They dance and then depart.*
Enter MEPHOSTOPHILIS.

FAU. What means this show? Speak, Mephostophilis.
MEPH. Nothing, Faustus, but to delight thy mind
　　And let thee see what magic can perform.
FAU. But may I raise such spirits when I please?
MEPH. Ay, Faustus, and do greater things than these.
FAU. Then, Mephostophilis, receive this scroll,
　　A deed of gift of body and of soul:
　　But yet conditionally that thou perform　　　　　　90
　　All covenants and articles between us both.
MEPH. Faustus, I swear by hell and Lucifer
　　To effect all promises between us made.
FAU. Then hear me read it, Mephostophilis.
　　On these conditions following:
　　　First, that Faustus may be a spirit in form and substance;
　　　Secondly, that Mephostophilis shall be his servant and at
　　his command;
　　　Thirdly, that Mephostophilis shall do for him and bring
　　him whatsoever;　　　　　　　　　　　　　　　　　　100
　　　Fourthly, that he shall be in his chamber or house invis-
　　ible;
　　　Lastly, that he shall appear to the said John Faustus at all
　　times in what form or shape soever he please;
　　　I, John Faustus of Wittenberg, doctor, by these presents
　　do give both body and soul to Lucifer, prince of the east, and
　　his minister Mephostophilis, and furthermore grant unto
　　them that, four-and-twenty years being expired, the articles
　　above written inviolate, full power to fetch or carry the said

　　83. *show:* pageant, procession.
　　90. *conditionally:* on condition.
　　91. *articles:* stipulations.
　　105. *these presents:* this present document (a legal term).
　　109. *inviolate:* not having been violated.

NOTES: p. 159

John Faustus, body and soul, flesh, blood, or goods, into their   110
habitation wheresoever.

By me John Faustus.

MEPH. Speak, Faustus, do you deliver this as your deed?

FAU. Ay, take it, and the devil give thee good on't!

MEPH. Now, Faustus, ask what thou wilt.

FAU. First will I question with thee about hell.

   Tell me, where is the place that men call hell?

MEPH. Under the heavens.

FAU. Ay, so are all things else; but whereabouts?

MEPH. Within the bowels of these elements,   120

   Where we are tortur'd and remain for ever.

   Hell hath no limits, nor is circumscrib'd

   In one self place, but where we are is hell,

   And where hell is, there must we ever be;

   And, to be short, when all the world dissolves

   And every creature shall be purify'd,

   All places shall be hell that is not heaven.

FAU. I think hell's a fable.

MEPH. Ay, think so still, till experience change thy mind.

FAU. Why, dost thou think that Faustus shall be damn'd?   130

MEPH. Ay, of necessity, for here's the scroll

   In which thou hast given thy soul to Lucifer.

FAU. Ay, and body too; but what of that?

   Think'st thou that Faustus is so fond to imagine

   That after this life there is any pain?

   No, these are trifles and mere old wives' tales.

MEPH. But I am an instance to prove the contrary,

   For I tell thee I am damn'd and now in hell.

FAU. Nay, and this be hell, I'll willingly be damn'd:

   What, sleeping, eating, walking, and disputing!   140

114. *on't:* of it.
116. *question with thee:* put questions to you.
120. *these elements:* the elements (earth, water, air, and fire).
122. *circumscrib'd:* bounded.
123. *one self place:* one and the same place.
134. *fond:* foolish.
139. *and:* if.

NOTES: p. 159

But, leaving this, let me have a wife, the fairest maid in
Germany, for I am wanton and lascivious and cannot live
without a wife.

MEPH. How, a wife! I prithee, Faustus, talk not of a wife.

FAU. Nay, sweet Mephostophilis, fetch me one, for I will have
one.

MEPH. Well, thou wilt have one. Sit there till I come; I'll fetch
thee a wife in the devil's name.   [*Exit.*]

Enter with a Devil *dressed like a woman,*
with fireworks.

Tell me, Faustus, how dost thou like thy wife?

FAU. Here's a hot whore indeed! No, I'll no wife.   150

MEPH. Marriage is but a ceremonial toy;
And if thou lov'st me, think no more of it.
I'll cull thee out the fairest courtesans
And bring them every morning to thy bed;
She whom thine eye shall like, thy heart shall have,
Were she as chaste as was Penelope,
As wise as Saba, or as beautiful
As was bright Lucifer before his fall.
Hold; take this book, peruse it thoroughly:
The iterating of these lines brings gold;   160
The framing of this circle on the ground
Brings thunder, whirlwinds, storm, and lightning;
Pronounce this thrice devoutly to thyself
And men in harness shall appear to thee,
Ready to execute what thou command'st.

FAU. Thanks, Mephostophilis; yet fain would I have a book
wherein I might behold all spells and incantations, that I
might raise up spirits when I please.

144. *prithee:* pray thee.
151. *ceremonial toy:* trifling ceremony.
152. *And if:* if (tautological, but more emphatic than 'and').
153. *cull:* choose.
160. *iterating:* repetition.
164. *harness:* armour.
166. *fain:* gladly.

NOTES: p. 160

MEPH. Here they are in this book.　　　*There turn to them.*

FAU. Now would I have a book where I might see all charac- 170
　　ters of planets of the heavens, that I might know their
　　motions and dispositions.

MEPH. Here they are, too.　　　*Turn to them.*

FAU. Nay, let me have one book more, and then I have done,
　　wherein I might see all plants, herbs, and trees that grow
　　upon the earth.

MEPH. Here they be.

FAU. O, thou art deceived.

MEPH. Tut, I warrant thee.　　　*Turn to them. Exeunt.*

[*Here a scene is probably lost. It may well have shown the Clown,
Robin, after stealing one of Faustus' books of magic, leaving
Wagner's service to become an ostler at an inn.*]

Scene VI

Enter FAUSTUS *in his study and* MEPHOSTOPHILIS.

FAU. When I behold the heavens, then I repent
　　And curse thee, wicked Mephostophilis,
　　Because thou hast depriv'd me of those joys.

MEPH. 'Twas thine own seeking, Faustus, thank thyself.
　　But think'st thou heaven is such a glorious thing?
　　I tell thee, Faustus, it is not half so fair
　　As thou or any man that breathes on earth.

FAU. How prov'st thou that?

MEPH. 'Twas made for man; then he's more excellent.

FAU. If heaven was made for man, 'twas made for me: 　　10
　　I will renounce this magic and repent.

Enter the two Angels.

GOOD ANG. Faustus, repent; yet God will pity thee.

170–1. *characters:* symbols.
172. *dispositions:* situations (an astrological term).
12. *yet:* even now.

NOTES: p 160

BAD ANG. Thou art a spirit; God cannot pity thee.

FAU. Who buzzeth in mine ears I am a spirit?
Be I a devil, yet God may pity me;
Yea, God will pity me if I repent.

BAD ANG. Ay, but Faustus never shall repent.   *Exeunt* Angels.

FAU. My heart is harden'd, I cannot repent.
Scarce can I name salvation, faith, or heaven,
But fearful echoes thunders in mine ears,   20
'Faustus, thou art damn'd!' Then guns and knives,
Swords, poison, halters, and envenom'd steel
Are laid before me to dispatch myself;
And long ere this I should have done the deed
Had not sweet pleasure conquer'd deep despair.
Have not I made blind Homer sing to me
Of Alexander's love and Oenon's death?
And hath not he, that built the walls of Thebes
With ravishing sound of his melodious harp,
Made music with my Mephostophilis?   30
Why should I die, then, or basely despair?
I am resolv'd Faustus shall not repent. --
Come, Mephostophilis, let us dispute again,
And reason of divine astrology.
Speak, are there many spheres above the moon?
Are all celestial bodies but one globe
As is the substance of this centric earth?

MEPH. As are the elements, such are the heavens,
Even from the moon unto the empyreal orb,
Mutually folded in each other's spheres,   40
And jointly move upon one axle-tree,

13. *spirit:* evil spirit, devil.
14. *buzzeth:* mutters.
15. *Be I:* even if I am.
22. *halters:* hangman's ropes.
23. *dispatch:* kill.
34. *astrology:* astronomy applied to human uses.
35–68. For explanations of the astronomical and other scientific terms
occurring in this passage and not glossed here, see notes.
37. *centric:* central.

NOTES: pp. 160–1

Whose termine is term'd the world's wide pole;
Nor are the names of Saturn, Mars, or Jupiter
Feign'd, but are erring stars.

FAU.   But have they all
One motion, both *situ et tempore*?

MEPH. All move from east to west in four-and-twenty hours
upon the poles of the world, but differ in their motions
upon the poles of the zodiac.

FAU. These slender questions Wagner can decide:
Hath Mephostophilis no greater skill?   50
Who knows not the double motion of the planets?
That the first is finish'd in a natural day;
The second thus: Saturn in thirty years,
Jupiter in twelve, Mars in four, the sun, Venus, and Mer-
cury in a year, the moon in twenty-eight days. These are
freshmen's suppositions. But tell me, hath every sphere a
dominion or *intelligentia*?

MEPH. Ay.

FAU. How many heavens or spheres are there?

MEPH. Nine: the seven planets, the firmament, and the em-   60
pyreal heaven.

FAU. But is there not *coelum igneum? et crystallinum*?

MEPH. No, Faustus, they be but fables.

FAU. Resolve me then in this one question:
Why are not conjunctions, oppositions, aspects, eclipses
all at one time, but in some years we have more, in some
less?

MEPH. *Per inaequalem motum respectu totius.*

FAU. Well, I am answered. Now tell me who made the world.

MEPH. I will not.   70

FAU. Sweet Mephostophilis, tell me.

MEPH. Move me not, Faustus.

FAU. Villain, have not I bound thee to tell me any thing?

42. *termine:* end, extremity (a trisyllable).
49. *slender:* trifling.
64. *Resolve me:* bring me to clear understanding.
72. *Move:* anger.

NOTES: pp. 161–2

MEPH. Ay, that is not against our kingdom.
    This is. Thou art damn'd; think thou of hell.
FAU. Think, Faustus, upon God, that made the world.
MEPH. Remember this! *Exit.*
FAU. Ay, go, accursed spirit, to ugly hell!
    'Tis thou hast damn'd distressed Faustus' soul.
    Is't not too late? 80

Enter the two Angels.

BAD ANG. Too late.
GOOD ANG. Never too late, if Faustus will repent.
BAD ANG. If thou repent, devils will tear thee in pieces.
GOOD ANG. Repent, and they shall never raze thy skin.
Exeunt Angels.

FAU. O Christ, my saviour, my saviour,
    Help to save distressed Faustus' soul.

Enter LUCIFER, BEELZEBUB, *and* MEPHOSTOPHILIS.

LUC. Christ cannot save thy soul, for he is just;
    There's none but I have interest in the same.
FAU. O, what art thou that look'st so terribly?
LUC. I am Lucifer, 90
    And this is my companion prince in hell.
FAU. O Faustus, they are come to fetch thy soul.
BEEL. We are come to tell thee thou dost injure us.
LUC. Thou call'st on Christ contrary to thy promise.
BEEL. Thou shouldst not think on God.
LUC.   Think on the devil.
BEEL. And his dam too.
FAU. Nor will I henceforth; pardon me in this,
    And Faustus vows never to look to heaven,
    Never to name God or to pray to him,
    To burn his scriptures, slay his ministers, 100
    And make my spirits pull his churches down.

LUC. So shalt thou show thyself an obedient servant,
     And we will highly gratify thee for it.

BEEL. Faustus, we are come from hell in person to show thee
      some pastime. Sit down, and thou shalt behold the Seven
      Deadly Sins appear to thee in their own proper shapes
      and likeness.

FAU. That sight will be as pleasant to me as paradise was to
     Adam the first day of his creation.

LUC. Talk not of paradise or creation, but mark the show.   110
     Go, Mephostophilis, fetch them in.

Enter the Seven Deadly Sins [*led by a* Piper].

BEEL. Now, Faustus, question them of their names and dis-
      positions.

FAU. That shall I soon. What art thou, the first?

PRIDE. I am Pride. I disdain to have any parents. I am like
       to Ovid's flea; I can creep into every corner of a wench:
       sometimes, like a periwig, I sit upon her brow; next, like
       a necklace, I hang about her neck; then, like a fan of
       feathers, I kiss her lips; and then, turning myself to a
       wrought smock, do what I list. But fie, what a smell is   120
       here! I'll not speak another word, unless the ground be
       perfumed and covered with cloth of arras.

FAU. Thou art a proud knave indeed. What art thou, the
     second?

COVETOUSNESS. I am Covetousness, begotten of an old
       churl in a leather bag; and, might I now obtain my wish,
       this house, you and all, should turn to gold, that I might
       lock you safe into my chest. O my sweet gold!

FAU. And what art thou, the third?

103. *gratify:* reward.
106. *own proper:* own.
110. *show:* pageant, procession.
114. *soon:* at once.
117. *periwig:* wig.
120. *wrought:* embroidered.   *list:* please.
125, 130. *of:* by.
126. *churl:* miser.   *leather bag:* money-bag.

NOTES: p. 162

ENVY. I am Envy, begotten of a chimney-sweeper and an 130
oyster-wife. I cannot read and therefore wish all books
burned. I am lean with seeing others eat. O, that there
would come a famine over all the world, that all might
die, and I live alone! then thou shouldst see how fat I'd
be. But must thou sit and I stand? Come down, with a
vengeance!

FAU. Out, envious wretch! But what art thou, the fourth?

WRATH. I am Wrath. I had neither father nor mother; I
leaped out of a lion's mouth when I was scarce an hour
old, and ever since have run up and down the world with 140
these case of rapiers, wounding myself when I could get
none to fight withal. I was born in hell; and look to it, for
some of you shall be my father.

FAU. And what art thou, the fifth?

GLUTTONY. I am Gluttony. My parents are all dead, and the
devil a penny they have left me but a small pension, and
that buys me thirty meals a day and ten bevers – a small
trifle to suffice nature. I come of a royal pedigree: my
father was a gammon of bacon, and my mother was a
hogshead of claret wine; my godfathers were these, Peter 150
Pickled-herring and Martin Martlemas-beef. But my
godmother, O, she was a jolly gentlewoman, and well
beloved in every good town and city; her name was
Margery March-beer. Now, Faustus, thou hast heard
all my progeny; wilt thou bid me to supper?

FAU. No, I'll see thee hanged; thou wilt eat up all my vic-
tuals.

GLUT. Then the devil choke thee.

FAU. Choke thyself, glutton! What art thou, the sixth?

SLOTH. Heigh-ho! I am Sloth. I was begotten on a sunny 160
bank, where I have lain ever since; and you have done

135–6. *with a vengeance!* with a curse!
141. *these case of:* this pair of.
142. *withal:* with.
147. *bevers:* light snacks.
155. *progeny:* lineage.

NOTES: pp. 162–3

me great injury to bring me from thence: let me be carried thither again by Gluttony and Lechery. Heigh-ho!
I'll not speak a word more for a king's ransom.

FAU. And what are you, Mistress Minx, the seventh and last?

LECHERY. Who, I, sir? I am one that loves an inch of raw
mutton better than an ell of fried stockfish, and the first
letter of my name begins with Lechery.

LUC. Away, to hell, away! On, piper!

Exeunt the Seven Sins [*and the* Piper].

FAU. O, how this sight doth delight my soul!   170

LUC. But, Faustus, in hell is all manner of delight.

FAU. O, might I see hell and return again safe, how happy
were I then!

LUC. Faustus, thou shalt; at midnight I will send for thee.
Meanwhile peruse this book and view it throughly,
And thou shalt turn thyself into what shape thou wilt.

FAU. Thanks, mighty Lucifer.
This will I keep as chary as my life.

LUC. Now, Faustus, farewell.

FAU. Farewell, great Lucifer. Come, Mephostophilis.   180

Exeunt omnes several ways.

Scene VII

Enter the Clown [ROBIN].

ROB. What, Dick, look to the horses there till I come again. I
have gotten one of Doctor Faustus' conjuring books, and
now we'll have such knavery as 't passes.

Enter DICK.

162. *injury:* wrong.
167. *ell:* 45 inches.
stockfish: dried codfish.
175. *throughly:* thoroughly.
178. *chary:* carefully.
I. *again:* back.
3. *as 't passes:* as beats everything.

NOTES: p. 163

DICK. What, Robin, you must come away and walk the horses.

ROB. I walk the horses! I scorn 't, 'faith, I have other matters in hand; let the horses walk themselves and they will. [*Reading*] *A per se, a; t, h, e, the; o per se, o; deny orgon, gorgon.* Keep further from me, O thou illiterate and unlearned ostler.

DICK. 'Snails, what hast thou got there, a book? Why, thou 10 canst not tell ne'er a word on't.

ROB. That thou shalt see presently. Keep out of the circle, I say, lest I send you into the hostry with a vengeance.

DICK. That's like, 'faith! You had best leave your foolery, for an my master come he'll conjure you, 'faith.

ROB. My master conjure me! I'll tell thee what, an my master come here, I'll clap as fair a pair of horns on's head as e'er thou sawest in thy life.

DICK. Thou needest not do that, for my mistress hath done it.

ROB. Ay, there be of us here that have waded as deep into 20 matters as other men, if they were disposed to talk.

DICK. A plague take you! I thought you did not sneak up and down after her for nothing. But I prithee tell me in good sadness, Robin, is that a conjuring book?

ROB. Do but speak what thou'lt have me to do, and I'll do 't. If thou'lt dance naked, put off thy clothes, and I'll conjure thee about presently. Or if thou'lt go but to the tavern with me, I'll give thee white wine, red wine, claret wine,

6. *and:* if.
10. *'Snails:* by God's nails (an oath).
11. *on't:* of it.
12. *presently:* directly, at once.
13. *hostry:* inn, hostelry.
with a vengeance: with a curse!
14. *like:* probable (here spoken ironically).
15, 16. *an:* if.
17. *on's:* on his.
23. *prithee:* pray thee.
23–4. *in good sadness:* in earnest.
27. *presently:* directly, at once.
28. *claret wine:* wine of light red colour.

NOTES: pp. 163–4

sack, muscadine, malmsey, and whippincrust, hold-belly-
hold, and we'll not pay one penny for it.   30

DICK. O brave! prithee let's to it presently, for I am as dry as
a dog.

ROB. Come, then, let's away.   *Exeunt.*

Chorus I

Enter the Chorus.

CHO. Learned Faustus,
    To find the secrets of astronomy,
    Graven in the book of Jove's high firmament,
    Did mount him up to scale Olympus' top,
    Where, sitting in a chariot burning bright
    Drawn by the strength of yoked dragons' necks,
    He views the clouds, the planets, and the stars,
    The tropics, zones, and quarters of the sky,
    From the bright circle of the horned moon
    Even to the height of *primum mobile*;   10
    And, whirling round with this circumference
    Within the concave compass of the pole,
    From east to west his dragons swiftly glide
    And in eight days did bring him home again.
    Not long he stay'd within his quiet house
    To rest his bones after his weary toil,
    But new exploits do hale him out again,
    And, mounted then upon a dragon's back,

29. *sack:* strong light-coloured wine imported from Spain and the
Canaries.
    muscadine: muscatel.
    malmsey: another strong sweet wine.
29–30. *hold-belly-hold:* a belly-full.
31. *brave:* excellent, fine.
    prithee: I pray thee.
    let's: let us go.
    presently: immediately.
3. *firmament:* sphere of the fixed stars.
17. *hale:* draw.

NOTES: p. 164

That with his wings did part the subtle air,
He now is gone to prove cosmography,   20
That measures coasts and kingdoms of the earth,
And as I guess will first arrive at Rome
To see the Pope and manner of his court
And take some part of holy Peter's feast,
The which this day is highly solemniz'd.   *Exit.*

Scene VIII

Enter FAUSTUS *and* MEPHOSTOPHILIS.

FAU. Having now, my good Mephostophilis,
        Pass'd with delight the stately town of Trier,
        Environ'd round with airy mountain-tops,
        With walls of flint, and deep-entrenched lakes,
        Not to be won by any conquering prince;
        From Paris next, coasting the realm of France,
        We saw the river Main fall into Rhine,
        Whose banks are set with groves of fruitful vines;
        Then up to Naples, rich Campania,
        With buildings fair and gorgeous to the eye,   10
        Whose streets straight forth and pav'd with finest brick
        Quarters the town in four equivalents.
        There saw we learned Maro's golden tomb,
        The way he cut, an English mile in length,
        Thorough a rock of stone in one night's space.

19. *subtle:* tenuous, rarefied.
20. *prove:* put to the test.
cosmography: the science that maps the general features of the universe.
24. *take some part of:* share in.
25. *solemniz'd:* celebrated in due form.
4. *lakes:* moats.
6. *coasting:* passing along the side of.
11. *straight forth:* in straight lines.
12. *equivalents:* equal parts.
15. *Thorough:* through.

NOTES: pp. 164–5

From thence to Venice, Padua, and the rest,
In midst of which a sumptuous temple stands,
That threats the stars with her aspiring top,
Whose frame is pav'd with sundry colour'd stones
And roof'd aloft with curious work in gold.   20
Thus hitherto hath Faustus spent his time.
But tell me now, what resting-place is this?
Hast thou, as erst I did command,
Conducted me within the walls of Rome?

MEPH. I have, my Faustus, and for proof thereof
This is the goodly palace of the Pope,
And 'cause we are no common guests
I choose his privy chamber for our use.

FAU. I hope his Holiness will bid us welcome.

MEPH. All's one, for we'll be bold with his venison.   30
But now, my Faustus, that thou may'st perceive
What Rome contains for to delight thine eyes,
Know that this city stands upon seven hills
That underprop the groundwork of the same:
Just through the midst runs flowing Tiber's stream,
With winding banks that cut it in two parts,
Over the which four stately bridges lean,
That make safe passage to each part of Rome.
Upon the bridge call'd Ponte Angelo
Erected is a castle passing strong,   40
Where thou shalt see such store of ordinance
As that the double cannons forg'd of brass
Do match the number of the days contain'd
Within the compass of one complete year;
Beside the gates, and high pyramides
That Julius Caesar brought from Africa.

23. *erst:* not long ago.
28. *privy:* private.
34. *underprop the groundwork:* support the foundation.
37. *lean:* bend, incline.
40. *passing:* exceedingly.
41. *store:* abundance.   *ordinance:* artillery.
45. *Beside:* besides.

NOTES: p. 165

FAU. Now, by the kingdoms of infernal rule,
Of Styx, of Acheron, and the fiery lake
Of ever-burning Phlegethon, I swear
That I do long to see the monuments   50
And situation of bright-splendent Rome.
Come, therefore, let's away.

MEPH. Nay, stay, my Faustus; I know you'd see the Pope
And take some part of holy Peter's feast,
The which in state and high solemnity
This day is held through Rome and Italy
In honour of the Pope's triumphant victory.

FAU. Sweet Mephostophilis, thou pleasest me:
Whilst I am here on earth let me be cloy'd
With all things that delight the heart of man.   60
My four-and-twenty years of liberty
I'll spend in pleasure and in dalliance,
That Faustus' name, whilst this bright frame doth stand,
May be admired through the furthest land.

MEPH. 'Tis well said, Faustus; come, then, stand by me
And thou shalt see them come immediately.

FAU. Nay, stay, my gentle Mephostophilis,
And grant me my request, and then I go.
Thou know'st within the compass of eight days
We view'd the face of heaven, of earth, and hell.   70
So high our dragons soar'd into the air
That looking down the earth appear'd to me
No bigger than my hand in quantity.
There did we view the kingdoms of the world,
And what might please mine eye I there beheld.
Then in this show let me an actor be,
That this proud Pope may Faustus' cunning see.

51. *situation:* lay-out.
bright-splendent: brilliantly magnificent.
54. *take some part of:* share in.
62. *dalliance:* sport, play.
76. *show:* pageant, procession.
77, 81. *cunning:* skill.

NOTES: pp. 165–6

MEPH. Let it be so, my Faustus, but first stay
    And view their triumphs as they pass this way;
    And then devise what best contents thy mind,   80
    By cunning in thine art to cross the Pope
    Or dash the pride of this solemnity,
    To make his monks and abbots stand like apes
    And point like antics at his triple crown,
    To beat the beads about the friars' pates
    Or clap huge horns upon the cardinals' heads,
    Or any villainy thou canst devise,
    And I'll perform it, Faustus. Hark, they come!
    This day shall make thee be admir'd in Rome.

Enter the Cardinals *and* Bishops, *some bearing crosiers, some the
pillars;* Monks *and* Friars *singing their procession. Then the* Pope
and RAYMOND, KING OF HUNGARY, *with* BRUNO *led in chains.*

POPE. Cast down our footstool.
RAY.   Saxon Bruno, stoop,   90
    Whilst on thy back his Holiness ascends
    Saint Peter's chair and state pontifical.
BRU. Proud Lucifer, that state belongs to me:
    But thus I fall to Peter, not to thee.
POPE. To me and Peter shalt thou grovelling lie
    And crouch before the papal dignity:
    Sound trumpets, then, for thus Saint Peter's heir
    From Bruno's back ascends Saint Peter's chair.
                       A flourish while he ascends.
    Thus as the gods creep on with feet of wool
    Long ere with iron hands they punish men,   100
    So shall our sleeping vengeance now arise
    And smite with death thy hated enterprise.

79. *triumphs:* spectacular festivities.
84. *antics:* grotesques.
89. *admir'd:* wondered at.
Stage-direction: *procession:* form of prayer or worship sung in a religious
procession.
92, 93. *state:* throne.
98. Stage-direction: *flourish:* fanfare of trumpets.

NOTES: p. 166

Lord Cardinals of France and Padua,
Go forthwith to our holy consistory
And read amongst the statutes decretal
What, by the holy council held at Trent,
The sacred synod hath decreed for him
That doth assume the papal government
Without election and a true consent.
Away, and bring us word with speed.   110

I CARD. We go, my lord.   *Exeunt* Cardinals.

POPE. Lord Raymond –

FAU. Go, haste thee, gentle Mephostophilis,
Follow the cardinals to the consistory,
And, as they turn their superstitious books,
Strike them with sloth and drowsy idleness;
And make them sleep so sound that in their shapes
Thyself and I may parley with this Pope,
This proud confronter of the Emperor,
And in despite of all his holiness   120
Restore this Bruno to his liberty
And bear him to the states of Germany.

MEPH. Faustus, I go.

FAU.   Dispatch it soon:
The Pope shall curse that Faustus came to Rome.
                    Exeunt FAUSTUS *and* MEPHOSTOPHILIS.

BRU. Pope Adrian, let me have some right of law;
I was elected by the Emperor.

POPE. We will depose the Emperor for that deed
And curse the people that submit to him;
Both he and thou shalt stand excommunicate
And interdict from church's privilege   130
And all society of holy men.
He grows too proud in his authority,
Lifting his lofty head above the clouds,
And like a steeple overpeers the church.
But we'll pull down his haughty insolence;

107. *synod:* general council.
130. *interdict:* authoritatively cut off.

NOTES: pp. 166–7

And, as Pope Alexander, our progenitor,
Trod on the neck of German Frederick,
Adding this golden sentence to our praise,
'That Peter's heirs should tread on emperors
And walk upon the dreadful adder's back,   140
Treading the lion and the dragon down,
And fearless spurn the killing basilisk',
So will we quell that haughty schismatic
And by authority apostolical
Depose him from his regal government.
BRU. Pope Julius swore to princely Sigismund,
For him and the succeeding popes of Rome,
To hold the emperors their lawful lords.
POPE. Pope Julius did abuse the church's rights,
And therefore none of his decrees can stand.   150
Is not all power on earth bestow'd on us?
And therefore though we would we cannot err.
Behold this silver belt, whereto is fix'd
Seven golden keys fast seal'd with seven seals
In token of our sevenfold power from heaven,
To bind or loose, lock fast, condemn, or judge,
Resign or seal, or whatso pleaseth us.
Then he and thou and all the world shall stoop,
Or be assured of our dreadful curse
To light as heavy as the pains of hell.   160

Enter FAUSTUS *and* MEPHOSTOPHILIS *like the cardinals.*

MEPH. Now tell me, Faustus, are we not fitted well?
FAU. Yes, Mephostophilis, and two such cardinals
Ne'er serv'd a holy pope as we shall do.
But whilst they sleep within the consistory
Let us salute his reverend Fatherhood.
RAY. Behold, my lord, the cardinals are return'd.

136. *progenitor:* predecessor.
157. *Resign:* unseal.   *whatso:* whatever.
160. *light:* fall, descend.
161. *fitted:* prepared.
NOTES: p. 167

POPE. Welcome, grave fathers, answer presently,
　　　What have our holy council there decreed
　　　Concerning Bruno and the Emperor,
　　　In quittance of their late conspiracy   170
　　　Against our state and papal dignity?
FAU. Most sacred patron of the church of Rome,
　　　By full consent of all the synod
　　　Of priests and prelates, it is thus decreed:
　　　That Bruno and the German Emperor
　　　Be held as lollards and bold schismatics
　　　And proud disturbers of the church's peace.
　　　And if that Bruno by his own assent,
　　　Without enforcement of the German peers,
　　　Did seek to wear the triple diadem   180
　　　And by your death to climb Saint Peter's chair,
　　　The statutes decretal have thus decreed,
　　　He shall be straight condemn'd of heresy
　　　And on a pile of faggots burnt to death.
POPE. It is enough. Here, take him to your charge
　　　And bear him straight to Ponte Angelo,
　　　And in the strongest tower enclose him fast.
　　　Tomorrow, sitting in our consistory
　　　With all our college of grave cardinals,
　　　We will determine of his life or death.   190
　　　Here, take his triple crown along with you
　　　And leave it in the church's treasury.
　　　Make haste again, my good lord cardinals,
　　　And take our blessing apostolical.
MEPH. So, so; was never devil thus blest before.
FAU. Away, sweet Mephostophilis, be gone:
　　　The cardinals will be plagu'd for this anon.
　　　　　Exeunt FAUSTUS *and* MEPHOSTOPHILIS [*with* BRUNO].

167. *presently:* at once, directly.
170. *quittance of:* requital for.
171. *state:* settled government.
176. *lollards:* heretics.
179. *enforcement of:* compulsion by.

NOTES: p. 167

POPE. Go presently and bring a banquet forth,
    That we may solemnize Saint Peter's feast
    And with Lord Raymond, King of Hungary,   200
    Drink to our late and happy victory.   *Exeunt.*

Scene IX

The banquet is brought in; and then enter FAUSTUS *and*
MEPHOSTOPHILIS *in their own shapes.*

MEPH. Now, Faustus, come, prepare thyself for mirth:
    The sleepy cardinals are hard at hand
    To censure Bruno, that is posted hence,
    And on a proud-pac'd steed as swift as thought
    Flies o'er the Alps to fruitful Germany,
    There to salute the woeful Emperor.
FAU. The Pope will curse them for their sloth today,
    That slept both Bruno and his crown away.
    But now, that Faustus may delight his mind
    And by their folly make some merriment,   10
    Sweet Mephostophilis, so charm me here
    That I may walk invisible to all
    And do whate'er I please, unseen of any.
MEPH. Faustus, thou shalt; then kneel down presently,
        Whilst on thy head I lay my hand
        And charm thee with this magic wand.
        First wear this girdle, then appear
        Invisible to all are here:
        The planets seven, the gloomy air,
        Hell, and the Furies' forked hair,   20
        Pluto's blue fire, and Hecate's tree

198. *presently:* at once, directly.
199. *solemnize:* celebrate in due form.
3. *censure:* pronounce judgement upon.
posted: conveyed swiftly.
14. *presently:* at once, directly.
18. *all are:* all who are.

NOTES: p. 168

> *With magic spells so compass thee*
> *That no eye may thy body see.*

So, Faustus, now, for all their holiness,
Do what thou wilt, thou shalt not be discern'd.

FAU. Thanks, Mephostophilis; now, friars, take heed
Lest Faustus make your shaven crowns to bleed.

MEPH. Faustus, no more; see where the cardinals come.

Sound a sennet. Enter Pope *and all the* Lords. *Enter the*
Cardinals *with a book.*

POPE. Welcome, lord cardinals; come, sit down.
    Lord Raymond, take your seat. Friars, attend,   30
    And see that all things be in readiness,
    As best beseems this solemn festival.

I CARD. First, may it please your sacred Holiness
    To view the sentence of the reverend synod
    Concerning Bruno and the Emperor?

POPE. What needs this question? Did I not tell you
    Tomorrow we would sit i' th' consistory
    And there determine of his punishment?
    You brought us word even now, it was decreed
    That Bruno and the cursed Emperor   40
    Were by the holy council both condemn'd
    For loathed lollards and base schismatics:
    Then wherefore would you have me view that book?

I CARD. Your Grace mistakes; you gave us no such charge.

RAY. Deny it not; we all are witnesses
    That Bruno here was late deliver'd you,
    With his rich triple crown to be reserv'd
    And put into the church's treasury.

AMBO CARD. By holy Paul, we saw them not.

---

28. Stage-direction: *sennet:* set of notes on the trumpet announcing a ceremonial entrance.
  32. *beseems:* befits.
  42. *lollards:* heretics.
  47. *reserv'd:* preserved, kept safe.
  49. *Ambo Card.:* both cardinals.

NOTES: p. 168

POPE. By Peter, you shall die,   50
    Unless you bring them forth immediately.
    Hale them to prison, lade their limbs with gyves!
    False prelates, for this hateful treachery
    Curs'd be your souls to hellish misery.

                    [*Exeunt* Attendants *with the two* Cardinals.]

FAU. So, they are safe. Now, Faustus, to the feast:
    The Pope had never such a frolic guest.
POPE. Lord Archbishop of Rheims, sit down with us.
ARCH. I thank your Holiness.
FAU. Fall to, the devil choke you an you spare!
POPE. Who's that spoke? Friars, look about.   60
FRI. Here's nobody, if it like your Holiness.
POPE. Lord Raymond, pray fall to: I am beholding
    To the Bishop of Milan for this so rare a present.
FAU. I thank you, sir.   *Snatch it.*
POPE. How now! Who snatch'd the meat from me?
    Villains, why speak you not? –
    My good Lord Archbishop, here's a most dainty dish
    Was sent me from a cardinal in France.
FAU. I'll have that too.   [*Snatch it.*]
POPE. What lollards do attend our Holiness   70
    That we receive such great indignity?
    Fetch me some wine.
FAU. Ay, pray do, for Faustus is adry.
POPE. Lord Raymond, I drink unto your Grace.
FAU. I pledge your Grace.   [*Snatch it.*]
POPE. My wine gone too? Ye lubbers, look about
    And find the man that doth this villainy,

        52. *Hale:* drag.   *lade:* load.   *gyves:* fetters.
        56. *frolic:* sportive.
        61. *like:* please.
        62. *beholding:* indebted.
        68. *Was:* which was.
        70. *lollards:* heretics.
        73. *adry:* dry, thirsty.
        75. *pledge:* drink to.
        76. *lubbers:* clumsy, stupid fellows.

                    NOTES: p. 168

Or by our sanctitude you all shall die. –
I pray, my lords, have patience at this
Troublesome banquet.   80

ARCH. Please it your Holiness, I think it be
Some ghost crept out of purgatory, and now
Is come unto your Holiness for his pardon.

POPE. It may be so:
Go, then, command our priests to sing a dirge
To lay the fury of this same troublesome ghost. –
Once again, my lord, fall to.   *The* Pope *crosseth himself.*

FAU. How now?
Must every bit be spiced with a cross?
Well, use that trick no more, I would advise you. *Cross again.*
Well, there's the second time; aware the third: 91
I give you fair warning.   *Cross again.*
              Nay, then, take that!
            FAUSTUS *hits him a box of the ear.*

POPE. O, I am slain! help me, my lords;
O, come and help to bear my body hence.
Damn'd be this soul for ever for this deed.
                  Exeunt the Pope *and his train.*

MEPH. Now, Faustus, what will you do now? for I can tell you
you'll be cursed with bell, book, and candle.

FAU. Bell, book, and candle; candle, book, and bell;
Forward and backward, to curse Faustus to hell!

Enter the Friars, *with bell, book, and candle, for the dirge.*

1 FRI. Come, brethren, let's about our business with good   100
devotion.   *Sing this.*
       Cursed be he that stole his Holiness' meat from the table.
             Maledicat Dominus!
       Cursed be he that struck his Holiness a blow on the face.
             Maledicat Dominus!

       83. *pardon:* indulgence.
       85. *dirge:* requiem mass.
       86. *lay:* calm.   *fury:* importunity.
       91. *aware:* beware.

> *Cursed be he that took Friar Sandelo a blow on the pate.*
> *Maledicat Dominus!*
> *Cursed be he that disturbeth our holy dirge.*
> *Maledicat Donmius!*
> *Cursed be he that took away his Holiness' wine.*   110
> *Maledicat Dominus!*
> *Et omnes sancti! Amen.*

[FAUSTUS *and* MEPHOSTOPHILIS] *beat the* Friars, *and fling fireworks among them, and so exeunt.*

Scene X

Enter Clown [ROBIN] *and* DICK *with a cup.*

DICK. Sirrah Robin, we were best look that your devil can answer the stealing of this same cup, for the vintner's boy follows us at the hard heels.

ROB. 'Tis no matter, let him come! An he follow us, I'll so conjure him as he was never conjured in his life, I warrant him. Let me see the cup.

Enter Vintner.

DICK. Here 'tis. Yonder he comes. Now, Robin, now or never show thy cunning.

VINT. O, are you here? I am glad I have found you. You are a couple of fine companions! Pray, where's the cup you   10
stole from the tavern?

ROB. How, how? we steal a cup! Take heed what you say; we look not like cup-stealers, I can tell you.

VINT. Never deny't, for I know you have it, and I'll search you.

ROB. Search me? Ay, and spare not. [*Aside to Dick*] Hold the

106. *took:* gave.
2, 28–9, etc. *vintner:* innkeeper selling wine.
3. *boy:* servant.
at the hard heels: right at our heels.
4. *An:* if.
8. *cunning:* skill.
10. *companions:* fellows (here used contemptuously).

NOTES: p. 168

cup, Dick. [*To the Vintner*] Come, come, search me,
search me.   [Vintner *searches him.*]

VINT. [*To Dick*] Come on, sirrah, let me search you now.

DICK. Ay, ay, do, do. [*Aside to Robin*] Hold the cup, Robin.
[*To the Vintner*] I fear not your searching; we scorn to   20
steal your cups, I can tell you.   [Vintner *searches him.*]

VINT. Never outface me for the matter, for sure the cup is between you two.

ROB. Nay, there you lie; 'tis beyond us both.

VINT. A plague take you! I thought 'twas your knavery to take
it away. Come, give it me again.

ROB. Ay, much! when, can you tell? Dick, make me a circle,
and stand close at my back, and stir not for thy life. Vintner, you shall have your cup anon. Say nothing, Dick.
O per se, o; Demogorgon, Belcher, and Mephostophilis!   30

Enter MEPHOSTOPHILIS.

MEPH. You princely legions of infernal rule,
How am I vexed by these villains' charms!
From Constantinople have they brought me now
Only for pleasure of these damned slaves.   [*Exit* Vintner.]

ROB. By lady, sir, you have had a shrewd journey of it. Will it
please you to take a shoulder of mutton to supper, and a
tester in your purse, and go back again?

DICK. Ay, I pray you heartily, sir; for we called you but in jest,
I promise you.

MEPH. To purge the rashness of this cursed deed,   40
First be thou turned to this ugly shape,
For apish deeds transformed to an ape.

ROB. O brave, an ape! I pray, sir, let me have the carrying of
him about to show some tricks.

26. *again:* back.   29. *anon:* at once.
32. *villains:* low fellows.
35. *shrewd:* poor, unsatisfactory.
36. *to supper:* for supper.
37. *tester:* sixpence (a slang term).
42. *apish:* fantastically foolish.
43. *brave:* excellent, fine.

NOTES: p. 169

MEPH. And so thou shalt: be thou transformed to a dog, and
    carry him upon thy back. Away, be gone!

ROB. A dog! that's excellent: let the maids look well to their
    porridge-pots, for I'll into the kitchen presently. Come,
    Dick, come.   *Exeunt the two* Clowns.

MEPH. Now with the flames of ever-burning fire   50
    I'll wing myself and forthwith fly amain
    Unto my Faustus, to the Great Turk's court.   *Exit.*

Chorus 2

Enter Chorus.

CHO. When Faustus had with pleasure ta'en the view
    Of rarest things and royal courts of kings,
    He stay'd his course and so returned home,
    Where such as bare his absence but with grief –
    I mean his friends and nearest companions –
    Did gratulate his safety with kind words;
    And in their conference of what befell
    Touching his journey through the world and air
    They put forth questions of astrology,
    Which Faustus answer'd with such learned skill   10
    As they admir'd and wonder'd at his wit.
    Now is his fame spread forth in every land:
    Amongst the rest the Emperor is one,
    Carolus the Fifth, at whose palace now
    Faustus is feasted 'mongst his noblemen.
    What there he did in trial of his art
    I leave untold, your eyes shall see perform'd.   *Exit.*

48. *presently:* directly, at once.
51. *amain:* at full speed.
3. *stay'd his course:* stopped his travelling.
4. *but:* only.
6. *gratulate:* express joy at.
7. *conference:* talk.
9. *of astrology:* on astronomy.
11. *wit:* understanding.
16. *in trial of:* by way of experiment in.

NOTES: p. 169

Scene XI

Enter MARTINO *and* FREDERICK *at several doors.*

MAR. What ho, officers, gentlemen!
　　Hie to the presence to attend the Emperor.
　　Good Frederick, see the rooms be voided straight,
　　His Majesty is coming to the hall;
　　Go back, and see the state in readiness.

FRE. But where is Bruno, our elected Pope,
　　That on a fury's back came post from Rome?
　　Will not his Grace consort the Emperor?

MAR. O yes, and with him comes the German conjuror,
　　The learned Faustus, fame of Wittenberg,　　　　10
　　The wonder of the world for magic art;
　　And he intends to show great Carolus
　　The race of all his stout progenitors,
　　And bring in presence of his Majesty
　　The royal shapes and warlike semblances
　　Of Alexander and his beauteous paramour.

FRE. Where is Benvolio?

MAR. 　　　　　　　　Fast asleep, I warrant you.
　　He took his rouse with stoups of Rhenish wine
　　So kindly yesternight to Bruno's health
　　That all this day the sluggard keeps his bed.　　　20

FRE. See, see, his window's ope; we'll call to him.

MAR. What ho, Benvolio!

xi. Stage-direction: *several:* different.
2. *Hie:* go quickly.
presence: presence-chamber.
3. *voided straight:* cleared at once.
5. *state:* throne.
7. *post:* in haste.
8. *consort:* accompany.
10. *fame:* the glory.
15. *semblances:* appearances.
18. *took his rouse:* had a drinking-bout.
stoups: measures.

NOTES: p. 169

Enter BENVOLIO *above at a window, in his nightcap,*
buttoning.

BEN. What a devil ail you two?

MAR. Speak softly, sir, lest the devil hear you;
   For Faustus at the court is late arriv'd,
   And at his heels a thousand furies wait
   To accomplish whatsoever the doctor please.

BEN. What of this?

MAR. Come, leave thy chamber first, and thou shalt see
   This conjuror perform such rare exploits   30
   Before the Pope and royal Emperor
   As never yet was seen in Germany.

BEN. Has not the Pope enough of conjuring yet?
   He was upon the devil's back late enough;
   And if he be so far in love with him
   I would he would post with him to Rome again.

FRE. Speak, wilt thou come and see this sport?

BEN.   Not I.

MAR. Wilt thou stand in thy window and see it then?

BEN. Ay, and I fall not asleep i' th' meantime.

MAR. The Emperor is at hand, who comes to see   40
   What wonders by black spells may compass'd be.

BEN. Well, go you attend the Emperor. I am content for this
   once to thrust my head out at a window, for they say if a
   man be drunk overnight the devil cannot hurt him in the
   morning. If that be true, I have a charm in my head shall
   control him as well as the conjuror, I warrant you.

                    [*Exeunt* FREDERICK *and* MARTINO.]

        36. *post:* hasten.
        39. *and:* if.
        41. *compass'd:* accomplished, brought about.
        46. *control:* overpower.
                NOTES: pp. 169–70

Scene XII

A sennet. CHARLES *the* GERMAN EMPEROR, BRUNO, [DUKE OF]
SAXONY, FAUSTUS, MEPHOSTOPHILIS, FREDERICK, MARTINO,
and Attendants. [BENVOLIO *remains at his window.*]

EMP. Wonder of men, renown'd magician,
    Thrice-learned Faustus, welcome to our court.
    This deed of thine, in setting Bruno free
    From his and our professed enemy,
    Shall add more excellence unto thine art
    Than if by powerful necromantic spells
    Thou couldst command the world's obedience.
    For ever be belov'd of Carolus;
    And if this Bruno thou hast late redeem'd
    In peace possess the triple diadem   10
    And sit in Peter's chair despite of chance,
    Thou shalt be famous through all Italy
    And honour'd of the German Emperor.
FAU. These gracious words, most royal Carolus,
    Shall make poor Faustus to his utmost power
    Both love and serve the German Emperor
    And lay his life at holy Bruno's feet.
    For proof whereof, if so your Grace be pleas'd,
    The doctor stands prepar'd by power of art
    To cast his magic charms, that shall pierce through   20
    The ebon gates of ever-burning hell
    And hale the stubborn furies from their caves
    To compass whatsoe'er your Grace commands.

   xii. Stage-direction: *sennet:* set of notes on the trumpet announcing a
ceremonial entrance.
   4. *professed:* openly declared.
   5. *excellence:* dignity.
   9. *redeem'd:* set free.
   21. *ebon:* ebony.
   22. *hale:* drag.
   23. *compass:* accomplish, bring about.

NOTES: p. 170

BEN. Blood! he speaks terribly. But, for all that, I do not
     greatly believe him; he looks as like a conjuror as the Pope
     to a costermonger.

EMP. Then, Faustus, as thou late didst promise us,
     We would behold that famous conqueror,
     Great Alexander, and his paramour
     In their true shapes and state majestical   30
     That we may wonder at their excellence.

FAU. Your Majesty shall see them presently. –
     Mephostophilis, away,
     And with a solemn noise of trumpets' sound
     Present before this royal Emperor
     Great Alexander and his beauteous paramour.

MEPH. Faustus, I will.   *Exit* MEPHOSTOPHILIS.

BEN. Well, master doctor, an your devils come not away quick-
     ly, you shall have me asleep presently. Zounds, I could eat
     myself for anger to think I have been such an ass all this   40
     while to stand gaping after the devil's governor, and can
     see nothing.

FAU. I'll make you feel something anon, if my art fail me not. –
     My lord, I must forewarn your Majesty
     That when my spirits present the royal shapes
     Of Alexander and his paramour
     Your Grace demand no questions of the King,
     But in dumb silence let them come and go.

EMP. Be it as Faustus please; we are content.

BEN. Ay, ay, and I am content too. And thou bring Alexander   50
     and his paramour before the Emperor, I'll be Actaeon and
     turn myself to a stag.

FAU. And I'll play Diana and send you the horns presently.

24. *Blood!* by God's blood (an oath).
32, 39. *presently:* directly.
38. *an:* if.
39, 83, etc. *Zounds:* by God's wounds (an oath).
41. *governor:* tutor.
43. *anon:* before long.
50. *And:* if.

NOTES: p. 170

Sennet. Enter at one door the EMPEROR ALEXANDER, *at the other*
DARIUS; *they meet;* DARIUS *is thrown down;* ALEXANDER *kills him,*
takes off his crown, and, offering to go out, his Paramour *meets him;*
he embraceth her and sets DARIUS' *crown upon her head; and coming*
back both salute the Emperor, *who, leaving his state, offers to embrace*
them, which FAUSTUS *seeing suddenly stays him. Then trumpets cease*
and music sounds.

My gracious lord, you do forget yourself;
These are but shadows, not substantial.

EMP. O, pardon me, my thoughts are ravish'd so
With sight of this renowned Emperor
That in mine arms I would have compass'd him.
But, Faustus, since I may not speak to them
To satisfy my longing thoughts at full,   60
Let me this tell thee: I have heard it said
That this fair lady, whilst she liv'd on earth,
Had on her neck a little wart or mole;
How may I prove that saying to be true?

FAU. Your Majesty may boldly go and see.

EMP. Faustus, I see it plain,
And in this sight thou better pleasest me
Than if I gain'd another monarchy.

FAU. Away, be gone!   *Exit* Show.
See, see, my gracious lord, what strange beast is yon, that   70
thrusts his head out at the window.

EMP. O, wondrous sight! See, Duke of Saxony,
Two spreading horns most strangely fastened
Upon the head of young Benvolio.

SAX. What, is he asleep, or dead?

FAU. He sleeps, my lord, but dreams not of his horns.

EMP. This sport is excellent: we'll call and wake him.
What ho, Benvolio!

53. Stage-direction: *Sennet:* set of notes on the trumpet announcing a
ceremonial entrance.
   state: throne.   *stays:* stops.
58. *compass'd:* embraced.
70. *yon:* that.

NOTES: p. 170

BEN. A plague upon you! let me sleep awhile.

EMP. I blame thee not to sleep much, having such a head of   80
    thine own.

SAX. Look up, Benvolio, 'tis the Emperor calls.

BEN. The Emperor! where? O, zounds, my head!

EMP. Nay, and thy horns hold, 'tis no matter for thy head, for
    that's armed sufficiently.

FAU. Why, how now, sir knight? what, hanged by the horns?
    This is most horrible. Fie, fie, pull in your head for shame,
    let not all the world wonder at you.

BEN. Zounds, doctor, is this your villainy?

FAU. O, say not so, sir: the doctor has no skill,   90
    No art, no cunning to present these lords
    Or bring before this royal Emperor
    The mighty monarch, warlike Alexander.
    If Faustus do it, you are straight resolv'd
    In bold Actaeon's shape to turn a stag.
    And therefore, my lord, so please your Majesty,
    I'll raise a kennel of hounds shall hunt him so
    As all his footmanship shall scarce prevail
    To keep his carcase from their bloody fangs.
    Ho, Belimote, Argiron, Asterote!   100

BEN. Hold, hold! Zounds, he'll raise up a kennel of devils, I
    think, anon. Good my lord, entreat for me. 'Sblood, I
    am never able to endure these torments.

EMP. Then, good master doctor,
    Let me entreat you to remove his horns;
    He has done penance now sufficiently.

FAU. My gracious lord, not so much for injury done to me,

        84. *and:* if.
        91. *cunning:* ability.
        97. *shall:* which shall.
        98. *footmanship:* skill in running.
        101. *Hold, hold!* stop, stop!
        102. *anon:* directly.
        entreat: plead.
        102, 113. *'Sblood:* by God's blood (an oath).
        107. *injury:* wrong.

NOTES: pp. 170–1

as to delight your Majesty with some mirth, hath Faustus justly requited this injurious knight; which being all
I desire, I am content to remove his horns. – Mephosto-   110
philis, transform him. – And hereafter, sir, look you
speak well of scholars.

BEN. [*Aside*] Speak well of ye! 'Sblood, and scholars be such
cuckold-makers to clap horns of honest men's heads o'
this order, I'll ne'er trust smooth faces and small ruffs
more. But, an I be not revenged for this, would I might
be turned to a gaping oyster and drink nothing but salt
water.

EMP. Come, Faustus, while the Emperor lives,
In recompense of this thy high desert,   120
Thou shalt command the state of Germany
And live belov'd of mighty Carolus.   *Exeunt omnes.*

Scene XIII

Enter BENVOLIO, MARTINO, FREDERICK, *and* Soldiers.

MAR. Nay, sweet Benvolio, let us sway thy thoughts
From this attempt against the conjuror.
BEN. Away, you love me not, to urge me thus.
Shall I let slip so great an injury,
When every servile groom jests at my wrongs
And in their rustic gambols proudly say,
'Benvolio's head was grac'd with horns today'?
O, may these eyelids never close again
Till with my sword I have that conjuror slain.
If you will aid me in this enterprise,   10

109. *injurious:* insulting.
113. *and:* if.
114. *of:* on.
114–15. *o' this order:* in this fashion.
116. *an:* if.
4. *let slip:* overlook.
injury: wrong.
5. *groom:* low fellow.

Then draw your weapons and be resolute:
If not, depart: here will Benvolio die
But Faustus' death shall quit my infamy.

FRE. Nay, we will stay with thee, betide what may,
And kill that doctor if he come this way.

BEN. Then, gentle Frederick, hie thee to the grove
And place our servants and our followers
Close in an ambush there behind the trees.
By this, I know, the conjuror is near:
I saw him kneel and kiss the Emperor's hand   20
And take his leave laden with rich rewards.
Then, soldiers, boldly fight; if Faustus die,
Take you the wealth, leave us the victory.

FRE. Come, soldiers, follow me unto the grove:
Who kills him shall have gold and endless love.

Exit FREDERICK *with the* Soldiers.

BEN. My head is lighter than it was by th' horns,
But yet my heart's more ponderous than my head
And pants until I see that conjuror dead.

MAR. Where shall we place ourselves, Benvolio?

BEN. Here will we stay to bide the first assault.   30
O, were that damned hell-hound but in place,
Thou soon shouldst see me quit my foul disgrace.

Enter FREDERICK.

FRE. Close, close! the conjuror is at hand
And all alone comes walking in his gown;
Be ready then and strike the peasant down.

---

13. *But:* unless.
quit: repay, make a return for.
14. *betide what may:* whatever happens.
16. *hie thee:* go quickly.
18. *Close:* hidden.
19. *By this:* by this time.
30. *bide:* face.
31. *in place:* on the spot.
32. *quit:* repay, make a return for.
33. *Close, close!* keep still, keep still!
35. *peasant:* low fellow, rascal.

BEN. Mine be that honour, then: now, sword, strike home;
 For horns he gave, I'll have his head anon.

Enter FAUSTUS *with the false head.*

MAR. See, see, he comes.
BEN.   No words; this blow ends all.
 Hell take his soul, his body thus must fall.   [*Strikes.*]
FAU. O!   40
FRE. Groan you, master doctor?
BEN. Break may his heart with groans. Dear Frederick, see,
 Thus will I end his griefs immediately.
MAR. Strike with a willing hand. His head is off.

     [*Strikes;* FAUSTUS' *head falls off.*]

BEN. The devil's dead; the furies now may laugh.
FRE. Was this that stern aspect, that awful frown,
 Made the grim monarch of infernal spirits
 Tremble and quake at his commanding charms?
MAR. Was this that damned head whose heart conspir'd
 Benvolio's shame before the Emperor?   50
BEN. Ay, that's the head, and here the body lies,
 Justly rewarded for his villainies.
FRE. Come, let's devise how we may add more shame
 To the black scandal of his hated name.
BEN. First, on his head, in quittance of my wrongs,
 I'll nail huge forked horns and let them hang
 Within the window where he yok'd me first,
 That all the world may see my just revenge.
MAR. What use shall we put his beard to?
BEN. We'll sell it to a chimney-sweeper: it will wear out ten   60
 birchen brooms, I warrant you.
FRE. What shall his eyes do?

      37. *anon:* directly.
      43. *griefs:* mischiefs.
      47. *Made:* which made.
      55. *quittance of:* requital for.
      57. *yok'd:* held fast as with a yoke.

       NOTES: p. 171

BEN. We'll put out his eyes, and they shall serve for buttons
    to his lips to keep his tongue from catching cold.

MAR. An excellent policy. And now, sirs, having divided him,
    what shall the body do?   [FAUSTUS *gets up*.]

BEN. Zounds, the devil's alive again!

FRE. Give him his head, for God's sake!

FAU. Nay, keep it; Faustus will have heads and hands,
    Ay, all your hearts, to recompense this deed.   70
    Knew you not, traitors, I was limited
    For four-and-twenty years to breathe on earth?
    And had you cut my body with your swords,
    Or hew'd this flesh and bones as small as sand,
    Yet in a minute had my spirit return'd
    And I had breath'd a man made free from harm.
    But wherefore do I dally my revenge?
    Asteroth, Belimoth, Mephostophilis!

Enter MEPHOSTOPHILIS *and other* Devils.

Go, horse these traitors on your fiery backs
And mount aloft with them as high as heaven;   80
Thence pitch them headlong to the lowest hell.
Yet stay, the world shall see their misery,
And hell shall after plague their treachery.
Go, Belimoth, and take this caitiff hence
And hurl him in some lake of mud and dirt;
Take thou this other, drag him through the woods,
Amongst the pricking thorns and sharpest briers,
Whilst with my gentle Mephostophilis
This traitor flies unto some steepy rock
That rolling down may break the villain's bones   90
As he intended to dismember me.

> 65. *policy:* device, trick.
> 67. *Zounds:* by God's wounds (an oath).
> 77. *dally:* trifle with.
> 84. *caitiff:* despicable wretch.
> 89. *steepy:* precipitous.

NOTES: p. 171

Fly hence, dispatch my charge immediately.

FRE. Pity us, gentle Faustus, save our lives!

FAU. Away!

FRE.   He must needs go that the devil drives.

Exeunt Spirits *with the* Knights.

Enter the ambushed Soldiers.

1 SOLD. Come, sirs, prepare yourselves in readiness,
     Make haste to help these noble gentlemen;
     I heard them parley with the conjuror.

2 SOLD. See where he comes; dispatch, and kill the slave.

FAU. What's here? an ambush to betray my life!
     Then, Faustus, try thy skill. Base peasants, stand!   100
     For lo, these trees remove at my command
     And stand as bulwarks 'twixt yourselves and me
     To shield me from your hated treachery:
     Yet to encounter this your weak attempt
     Behold an army comes incontinent.

FAUSTUS *strikes the door, and enter a* Devil *playing on a drum, after him another bearing an ensign, and divers with weapons;* MEPHOSTO-PHILIS *with fireworks; they set upon the* Soldiers *and drive them out.*

[*Exit* FAUSTUS.]

Scene XIV

Enter at several doors BENVOLIO, FREDERICK, *and* MARTINO, *their heads and faces bloody, and besmeared with mud and dirt, all having horns on their heads.*

MAR. What ho, Benvolio!

BEN.   Here! What, Frederick, ho!

FRE. O help me, gentle friend. Where is Martino?

MAR. Dear Frederick, here,

100. *peasants:* low fellows, rascals.
101. *remove:* change their places.
105. *incontinent:* immediately.
Stage-direction: *divers:* several.
 xiv. Stage-direction: *several:* different.

NOTES: p. 171

Half smother'd in a lake of mud and dirt,
Through which the furies dragg'd me by the heels.

FRE. Martino, see! Benvolio's horns again.

MAR. O misery! How now, Benvolio?

BEN. Defend me, heaven, shall I be haunted still?

MAR. Nay, fear not, man, we have no power to kill.

BEN. My friends transformed thus! O hellish spite,   10
Your heads are all set with horns.

FRE.   You hit it right:
It is your own you mean, feel on your head.

BEN. Zounds, horns again!

MAR.   Nay, chafe not, man, we all are sped.

BEN. What devil attends this damn'd magician,
That, spite of spite, our wrongs are doubled?

FRE. What may we do that we may hide our shames?

BEN. If we should follow him to work revenge,
He'd join long asses' ears to these huge horns
And make us laughing-stocks to all the world.

MAR. What shall we then do, dear Benvolio?   20

BEN. I have a castle joining near these woods,
And thither we'll repair and live obscure
Till time shall alter these our brutish shapes.
Sith black disgrace hath thus eclips'd our fame,
We'll rather die with grief than live with shame.

Exeunt omnes.

13. *Zounds:* by God's wounds (an oath).
sped: done for (by being furnished with horns).
15. *spite of spite:* despite everything.
21. *joining near:* adjacent to.
24. *Sith:* seeing that.

NOTES: pp. 171–2

Scene XV

Enter FAUSTUS *and the* Horse-courser.

HOR. I beseech your worship, accept of these forty dollars.

FAU. Friend, thou canst not buy so good a horse for so small
a price. I have no great need to sell him; but if thou likest
him for ten dollars more, take him, because I see thou
hast a good mind to him.

HOR. I beseech you, sir, accept of this. I am a very poor man
and have lost very much of late by horse-flesh, and this
bargain will set me up again.

FAU. Well, I will not stand with thee; give me the money.
Now, sirrah, I must tell you that you may ride him o'er   10
hedge and ditch and spare him not; but, do you hear? in
any case ride him not into the water.

HOR. How, sir, not into the water? Why, will he not drink of
all waters?

FAU. Yes, he will drink of all waters. But ride him not into the
water; o'er hedge and ditch, or where thou wilt, but not
into the water. Go, bid the ostler deliver him unto you;
and remember what I say.

HOR. I warrant you, sir. O, joyful day! now am I a made man
for ever.   *Exit.*   20

FAU. What art thou, Faustus, but a man condemn'd to die?
Thy fatal time draws to a final end;
Despair doth drive distrust into my thoughts.
Confound these passions with a quiet sleep.
Tush, Christ did call the thief upon the cross;
Then rest thee, Faustus, quiet in conceit.   *He sits to sleep.*

Enter the Horse-courser, *wet.*

xv. Stage-direction, etc.: *Horse-courser:* horse-dealer.
9. *stand:* dispute, haggle.
22. *fatal time:* time allotted by fate.
25. *call:* offer salvation to.
26. *in conceit:* in mind.

NOTES: p. 172

HOR. O, what a cozening doctor was this! I, riding my horse
　　　into the water, thinking some hidden mystery had been
　　　in the horse, I had nothing under me but a little straw and
　　　had much ado to escape drowning. Well, I'll go rouse him　30
　　　and make him give me my forty dollars again. Ho, sirrah
　　　doctor, you cozening scab! Master doctor, awake, and
　　　rise, and give me my money again, for your horse is turned
　　　to a bottle of hay. Master doctor!　　　*He pulls off his leg.*
　　　Alas, I am undone! what shall I do? I have pulled off his
　　　leg.

FAU. O, help, help! the villain hath murdered me.

HOR. Murder or not murder, now he has but one leg I'll out-
　　　run him and cast this leg into some ditch or other.　　*[Exit.]*

FAU. Stop him, stop him, stop him! – Ha, ha, ha! Faustus　40
　　　hath his leg again, and the horse-courser a bundle of hay
　　　for his forty dollars.

Enter WAGNER.

How now, Wagner, what news with thee?

WAG. If it please you, the Duke of Vanholt doth earnestly en-
　　　treat your company and hath sent some of his men to
　　　attend you with provision fit for your journey.

FAU. The Duke of Vanholt's an honourable gentleman, and
　　　one to whom I must be no niggard of my cunning. Come
　　　away!　　　　　　　　　　　　　　　　　*Exeunt.*

Scene XVI

Enter Clown [ROBIN], DICK, Horse-courser, *and a* Carter.

CART. Come, my masters, I'll bring you to the best beer in
　　　Europe. What ho, hostess! Where be these whores?

　　　　　　27, 32. *cozening:* cheating.
　　　　　　31, 33. *again:* back.
　　　　　　32. *scab:* rascal, scoundrel.
　　　　　　34. *bottle:* bundle.
　　　　　　46. *provision fit:* all that is necessary.
　　　　　　　　　　NOTES: p. 172

Enter Hostess.

HOST. How now, what lack you? What, my old guests, wel-
    come.

ROB. Sirrah Dick, dost thou know why I stand so mute?

DICK. No, Robin, why is't?

ROB. I am eighteen pence on the score. But say nothing; see if
    she have forgotten me.

HOST. Who's this that stands so solemnly by himself? What,
    my old guest!   10

ROB. O, hostess, how do you? I hope my score stands still.

HOST. Ay, there's no doubt of that, for methinks you make no
    haste to wipe it out.

DICK. Why, hostess, I say, fetch us some beer.

HOST. You shall presently. Look up into th' hall there, ho! *Exit.*

DICK. Come, sirs, what shall we do now till mine hostess
    comes?

CART. Marry, sir, I'll tell you the bravest tale how a conjuror
    served me. You know Doctor Fauster?

HOR. Ay, a plague take him! Here's some on's have cause to   20
    know him. Did he conjure thee too?

CART. I'll tell you how he served me. As I was going to Witten-
    berg t'other day with a load of hay, he met me and asked
    me what he should give me for as much hay as he could
    eat. Now, sir, I, thinking that a little would serve his turn,
    bade him take as much as he would for three farthings. So
    he presently gave me my money and fell to eating; and, as
    I am a cursen man, he never left eating till he had eat up all
    my load of hay.

ALL. O monstrous, eat a whole load of hay!   30

ROB. Yes, yes, that may be, for I have heard of one that has eat
    a load of logs.

HOR. Now, sirs, you shall hear how villainously he served me.
    I went to him yesterday to buy a horse of him, and he

7. *on the score:* in debt.
18. *bravest:* finest.
27. *presently:* immediately.
    NOTES: pp. 172–3

would by no means sell him under forty dollars. So, sir, because I knew him to be such a horse as would run over hedge and ditch and never tire, I gave him his money. So, when I had my horse, Doctor Fauster bade me ride him night and day and spare him no time. 'But', quoth he, 'in any case ride him not into the water.' Now, sir, I, thinking 40 the horse had had some rare quality that he would not have me know of, what did I but rid him into a great river? and when I came just in the midst my horse vanished away, and I sat straddling upon a bottle of hay.

ALL. O brave doctor!

HOR. But you shall hear how bravely I served him for it. I went me home to his house, and there I found him asleep. I kept a hallooing and whooping in his ears, but all could not wake him. I, seeing that, took him by the leg and never rested pulling till I had pulled me his leg quite off; and 50 now 'tis at home in mine hostry.

DICK. And has the doctor but one leg then? That's excellent, for one of his devils turned me into the likeness of an ape's face.

CART. Some more drink, hostess!

ROB. Hark you, we'll into another room and drink awhile, and then we'll go seek out the doctor.   *Exeunt omnes.*

Scene XVII

Enter the DUKE OF VANHOLT, *his* DUCHESS, FAUSTUS, *and* MEPHOSTOPHILIS.

DUKE. Thanks, master doctor, for these pleasant sights.
Nor know I how sufficiently to recompense your great deserts in erecting that enchanted castle in the air, the sight whereof so delighted me,

44. *bottle:* bundle.
45. *brave:* excellent.
46. *bravely:* well.
51. *hostry:* inn, hostelry.

NOTES: p. 173

As nothing in the world could please me more.

FAU. I do think myself, my good lord, highly recompensed in
that it pleaseth your Grace to think but well of that which
Faustus hath performed. But, gracious lady, it may be
that you have taken no pleasure in those sights; therefore
I pray you tell me what is the thing you most desire to   10
have: be it in the world, it shall be yours. I have heard
that great-bellied women do long for things are rare and
dainty.

DUCH. True, master doctor, and, since I find you so kind, I
will make known unto you what my heart desires to have;
and were it now summer, as it is January, a dead time of
the winter, I would request no better meat than a dish of
ripe grapes.

FAU. This is but a small matter. Go, Mephostophilis, away!

                                   Exit MEPHOSTOPHILIS.

Madam, I will do more than this for your content.   20

Enter MEPHOSTOPHILIS *again with the grapes.*

Here, now taste ye these; they should be good,
For they come from a far country, I can tell you.

DUKE. This makes me wonder more than all the rest,
That at this time of the year, when every tree
Is barren of his fruit, from whence you had
These ripe grapes.

FAU. Please it your Grace, the year is divided into two circles
over the whole world, so that, when it is winter with us,
in the contrary circle it is likewise summer with them, as
in India, Saba, and such countries that lie far east, where   30
they have fruit twice a year. From whence, by means of a
swift spirit that I have, I had these grapes brought as you
see.

12. *great-bellied:* pregnant.
are: which are.
17. *meat:* food.
27. *circles:* hemispheres.
29. *likewise:* in the same manner.

NOTES: p. 173

DUCH. And, trust me, they are the sweetest grapes that e'er I
    tasted.   *The* Clowns *bounce at the gate within.*
DUKE. What rude disturbers have we at the gate?
    Go, pacify their fury, set it ope,
    And then demand of them what they would have.
            They knock again and call out to talk with FAUSTUS.
A SERVANT. Why, how now, masters, what a coil is there!
    What is the reason you disturb the Duke?   40
DICK. We have no reason for it, therefore a fig for him!
SER. Why, saucy varlets, dare you be so bold?
HOR. I hope, sir, we have wit enough to be more bold than
    welcome.
SER. It appears so: pray be bold elsewhere,
    And trouble not the Duke.
DUKE.   What would they have?
SER. They all cry out to speak with Doctor Faustus.
CART. Ay, and we will speak with him.
DUKE. Will you, sir? Commit the rascals.
DICK. Commit with us! He were as good commit with his   50
    father as commit with us.
FAU. I do beseech your Grace, let them come in;
    They are good subject for a merriment.
DUKE. Do as thou wilt, Faustus; I give thee leave.
FAU. I thank your Grace.

    Enter the Clown [ROBIN], DICK, Carter, *and* Horse-courser.

                    Why, how now, my good friends?
    'Faith, you are too outrageous; but come near,
    I have procur'd your pardons. Welcome all!
ROB. Nay, sir, we will be welcome for our money, and we will
    pay for what we take. What ho! give's half-a-dozen of
    beer here, and be hanged.   60

        35. Stage-direction: *bounce:* knock loudly.
        37. *fury:* importunity.
        39. *coil:* noisy disturbance, row.
        42. *varlets:* rascals.
        56. *outrageous:* violent.
                    NOTES: p. 173

FAU. Nay, hark you, can you tell me where you are?

CART. Ay, marry, can I; we are under heaven.

SER. Ay, but, sir sauce-box, know you in what place?

HOR. Ay, ay, the house is good enough to drink in. Zounds,
fill us some beer, or we'll break all the barrels in the house
and dash out all your brains with your bottles.

FAU. Be not so furious; come, you shall have beer.
My lord, beseech you give me leave awhile;
I'll gage my credit, 'twill content your Grace.

DUKE. With all my heart, kind doctor, please thyself;   70
Our servants and our court's at thy command.

FAU. I humbly thank your Grace. Then fetch some beer.

HOR. Ay, marry, there spake a doctor indeed; and, 'faith, I'll
drink a health to thy wooden leg for that word.

FAU. My wooden leg! what dost thou mean by that?

CART. Ha, ha, ha! Dost hear him, Dick? He has forgot his leg.

HOR. Ay, ay, he does not stand much upon that.

FAU. No, 'faith, not much upon a wooden leg.

CART. Good Lord, that flesh and blood should be so frail with
your worship! Do not you remember a horse-courser you   80
sold a horse to?

FAU. Yes, I remember I sold one a horse.

CART. And do you remember you bid he should not ride him
into the water?

FAU. Yes, I do very well remember that.

CART. And do you remember nothing of your leg?

FAU. No, in good sooth.

CART. Then I pray remember your curtsy.

FAU. I thank you, sir.

CART. 'Tis not so much worth. I pray you tell me one thing.   90

FAU. What's that?

CART. Be both your legs bedfellows every night together?

FAU. Wouldst thou make a colossus of me, that thou askest
me such questions?

64. *Zounds:* by God's wounds (an oath).
67. *furious:* importunate.
69. *gage:* stake.

NOTES: p. 174

CART. No, truly, sir, I would make nothing of you; but I
would fain know that.

Enter Hostess *with drink.*

FAU. Then I assure thee certainly they are.

CART. I thank you, I am fully satisfied.

FAU. But wherefore dost thou ask?

CART. For nothing, sir; but methinks you should have a   100
wooden bedfellow of one of 'em.

HOR. Why, do you hear, sir, did not I pull off one of your legs
when you were asleep?

FAU. But I have it again now I am awake: look you here, sir.

ALL. O horrible! Had the doctor three legs?

CART. Do you remember, sir, how you cozened me and eat
up my load of –   FAUSTUS *charms him dumb.*

DICK. Do you remember how you made me wear an ape's –
[FAUSTUS *charms him dumb.*]

HOR. You whoreson conjuring scab, do you remember how
you cozened me with a ho –   [FAUSTUS *charms him dumb.*]

ROB. Ha' you forgotten me? You think to carry it away with   111
your 'hey-pass' and 're-pass'. Do you remember the
dog's fa –   [FAUSTUS *charms him dumb.*] *Exeunt* Clowns.

HOST. Who pays for the ale? Hear you, master doctor, now
you have sent away my guests, I pray who shall pay me
for my a –   [FAUSTUS *charms her dumb.*] *Exit* Hostess.

DUCH. My lord,
We are much beholding to this learned man.

DUKE. So are we, madam, which we will recompense
With all the love and kindness that we may.   120
His artful sport drives all sad thoughts away.   *Exeunt.*

96. *fain:* gladly.
99. *wherefore:* for what purpose.
106, 110. *cozened:* cheated.
109. *scab:* rascal, scoundrel.
111. *carry it away:* carry it off, have the advantage.
118. *beholding:* obliged.

NOTES: p. 174

Scene XVIII

Thunder and lightning. Enter Devils *with covered dishes.* MEPHO-STOPHILIS *leads them into* FAUSTUS' *study. Then enter* WAGNER.

WAG. I think my master means to die shortly:
　　He has made his will and given me his wealth,
　　His house, his goods, and store of golden plate,
　　Besides two thousand ducats ready coin'd.
　　I wonder what he means. If death were nigh,
　　He would not banquet and carouse and swill
　　Amongst the students, as even now he doth,
　　Who are at supper with such belly-cheer
　　As Wagner ne'er beheld in all his life.
　　See where they come; belike the feast is ended.　　*Exit.*　10

　　　Enter FAUSTUS, MEPHOSTOPHILIS, *and two or three*
　　　　　　Scholars.

1 SCH. Master Doctor Faustus, since our conference about
　　fair ladies, which was the beautifullest in all the world, we
　　have determined with ourselves that Helen of Greece was
　　the admirablest lady that ever lived. Therefore, master
　　doctor, if you will do us that favour, as to let us see that
　　peerless dame of Greece, whom all the world admires for
　　majesty, we should think ourselves much beholding unto
　　you.

FAU. Gentlemen,
　　For that I know your friendship is unfeign'd,　　　　　20
　　And Faustus' custom is not to deny
　　The just requests of those that wish him well,
　　You shall behold that peerless dame of Greece,

　　　3. *store:* abundance.
　　　6. *carouse:* drink freely.
　　　7. *even now:* at this very moment.
　　　8. *belly-cheer:* gluttonous excess.
　　　11. *conference:* conversation.
　　　13. *determined with ourselves:* settled among ourselves.
　　　17. *beholding:* indebted.

NOTES: p. 174

No otherways for pomp and majesty
Than when Sir Paris cross'd the seas with her
And brought the spoils to rich Dardania.
Be silent, then, for danger is in words.

Music sounds. MEPHOSTOPHILIS *brings in* HELEN; *she passeth over the stage.*

2 SCH. Too simple is my wit to tell her praise
      Whom all the world admires for majesty.
3 SCH. No marvel though the angry Greeks pursu'd   30
      With ten years' war the rape of such a queen,
      Whose heavenly beauty passeth all compare.
1 SCH. Since we have seen the pride of nature's works
      And only paragon of excellence,
      Let us depart, and for this glorious deed
      Happy and blest be Faustus evermore.
FAU. Gentlemen, farewell; the same wish I to you.

                                        Exeunt Scholars.

                    Enter an Old Man.

OLD MAN. O gentle Faustus, leave this damned art,
      This magic, that will charm thy soul to hell
      And quite bereave thee of salvation.   40
      Though thou hast now offended like a man,
      Do not persever in it like a devil.
      Yet, yet, thou hast an amiable soul,
      If sin by custom grow not into nature:
      Then, Faustus, will repentance come too late,
      Then thou art banish'd from the sight of heaven;
      No mortal can express the pains of hell.
      It may be this my exhortation
      Seems harsh and all unpleasant; let it not,
      For, gentle son, I speak it not in wrath   50

      24. *otherways:* otherwise.
      30. *pursu'd:* campaigned to avenge.
      31. *rape:* abduction.
      32. *passeth all compare:* exceeds all comparison.
      34. *paragon:* pattern.

                    NOTES: p. 175

Or envy of thee, but in tender love
And pity of thy future misery;
And so have hope that this my kind rebuke,
Checking thy body, may amend thy soul.

FAU. Where art thou, Faustus? wretch, what hast thou done?
Damn'd art thou, Faustus, damn'd; despair and die!

                MEPHOSTOPHILIS *gives him a dagger.*

Hell claims his right and with a roaring voice
Says, 'Faustus, come; thine hour is almost come';
And Faustus now will come to do thee right.

                [FAUSTUS *goes to use the dagger.*]

OLD. O, stay, good Faustus, stay thy desperate steps!   60
I see an angel hovers o'er thy head
And with a vial full of precious grace
Offers to pour the same into thy soul:
Then call for mercy, and avoid despair.

FAU. O friend, I feel
Thy words to comfort my distressed soul.
Leave me awhile to ponder on my sins.

OLD. Faustus, I leave thee, but with grief of heart,
Fearing the enemy of thy hapless soul.   *Exit.*

FAU. Accursed Faustus, where is mercy now?   70
I do repent, and yet I do despair;
Hell strives with grace for conquest in my breast.
What shall I do to shun the snares of death?

MEPH. Thou traitor, Faustus, I arrest thy soul
For disobedience to my sovereign lord:
Revolt, or I'll in piecemeal tear thy flesh.

FAU. I do repent I e'er offended him.
Sweet Mephostophilis, entreat thy lord
To pardon my unjust presumption,

51. *envy of:* ill-will towards.
54. *Checking:* reproving.
57. *his right:* its rights.
59. *do thee right:* pay you your due.
61. *hovers:* who hovers.
76. *Revolt:* return to your allegiance.

NOTES: p. 175

And with my blood again I will confirm   80
The former vow I made to Lucifer.

MEPH. Do it, then, Faustus, with unfeigned heart,
Lest greater dangers do attend thy drift.

FAU. Torment, sweet friend, that base and aged man
That durst dissuade me from thy Lucifer,
With greatest torment that our hell affords.

MEPH. His faith is great; I cannot touch his soul;
But what I may afflict his body with
I will attempt, which is but little worth.

FAU. One thing, good servant, let me crave of thee   90
To glut the longing of my heart's desire:
That I may have unto my paramour
That heavenly Helen which I saw of late,
Whose sweet embraces may extinguish clear
Those thoughts that do dissuade me from my vow,
And keep mine oath I made to Lucifer.

MEPH. This or what else my Faustus shall desire
Shall be perform'd in twinkling of an eye.

Enter HELEN *again, passing over between two* Cupids.

FAU. Was this the face that launch'd a thousand ships
And burnt the topless towers of Ilium?   100
Sweet Helen, make me immortal with a kiss.
Her lips suck forth my soul: see where it flies!
Come, Helen, come, give me my soul again.
Here will I dwell, for heaven is in these lips,
And all is dross that is not Helena.

Enter Old Man.

I will be Paris, and for love of thee

83. *drift:* drifting, shilly-shallying.
91. *glut:* appease.
94. *clear:* entirely.
96. *keep:* preserve unbroken.
100. *topless:* immeasurably high.
103. *again:* back.

NOTES: pp. 175–6

Instead of Troy shall Wittenberg be sack'd,
And I will combat with weak Menelaus
And wear thy colours on my plumed crest,
Yea, I will wound Achilles in the heel   110
And then return to Helen for a kiss.
O, thou art fairer than the evening's air
Clad in the beauty of a thousand stars,
Brighter art thou than flaming Jupiter
When he appear'd to hapless Semele,
More lovely than the monarch of the sky
In wanton Arethusa's azur'd arms,
And none but thou shalt be my paramour.
                    Exeunt [FAUSTUS, HELEN, *and the* Cupids].
OLD MAN. Accursed Faustus, miserable man,
          That from thy soul exclud'st the grace of heaven   120
          And fliest the throne of his tribunal seat!

                    Enter the Devils.

Satan begins to sift me with his pride:
As in this furnace God shall try my faith,
My faith, vile hell, shall triumph over thee.
Ambitious fiends, see how the heavens smiles
At your repulse and laughs your state to scorn!
Hence, hell! for hence I fly unto my God.   *Exeunt.*

                    Scene XIX

Thunder. Enter LUCIFER, BEELZEBUB, *and* MEPHOSTOPHILIS
                    [*above*].

LUC. Thus from infernal Dis do we ascend
      To view the subjects of our monarchy,
      Those souls which sin seals the black sons of hell,
      'Mong which as chief, Faustus, we come to thee,

              109. *crest:* helmet.
              122. *sift:* test.   *pride:* display of power.
              126. *state:* power.
                    NOTES: p. 176

Bringing with us lasting damnation
To wait upon thy soul; the time is come
Which makes it forfeit.
MEPH.   And this gloomy night
Here in this room will wretched Faustus be.
BEEL. And here we'll stay
To mark him how he doth demean himself.   10
MEPH. How should he but in desperate lunacy?
Fond worldling, now his heart-blood dries with grief,
His conscience kills it, and his labouring brain
Begets a world of idle fantasies
To overreach the devil; but all in vain:
His store of pleasures must be sauc'd with pain.
He and his servant Wagner are at hand,
Both come from drawing Faustus' latest will.
See where they come.

Enter FAUSTUS *and* WAGNER.

FAU. Say, Wagner, thou hast perus'd my will: 20
How dost thou like it?
WAG.   Sir, so wondrous well
As in all humble duty I do yield
My life and lasting service for your love.

Enter the Scholars.

FAU. Gramercies, Wagner. Welcome, gentlemen. [*Exit* WAGNER.]
1 SCH. Now, worthy Faustus, methinks your looks are changed.
FAU. Ah, gentlemen!
2 SCH. What ails Faustus?
FAU. Ah, my sweet chamber-fellow, had I lived with thee,
then had I lived still, but now must die eternally. Look,
sirs, comes he not? comes he not?   30
1 SCH. O my dear Faustus, what imports this fear?

10. *demean himself:* behave.
16. *sauc'd with:* paid for dearly with.
24. *Gramercies:* thank you.
31. *imports:* is the meaning of.

NOTES: p. 177

2 SCH. Is all our pleasure turned to melancholy?

3 SCH. He is not well with being over-solitary.

2 SCH. If it be so, we'll have physicians, and Faustus shall be
cured.

3 SCH. 'Tis but a surfeit, sir; fear nothing.

FAU. A surfeit of deadly sin, that hath damned both body and
soul.

2 SCH. Yet, Faustus, look up to heaven and remember God's
mercy is infinite.   40

FAU. But Faustus' offence can ne'er be pardoned: the serpent
that tempted Eve may be saved, but not Faustus. Ah,
gentlemen, hear me with patience, and tremble not at my
speeches. Though my heart pants and quivers to remember that I have been a student here these thirty years, O,
would I had never seen Wittenberg, never read book! and
what wonders I have done all Germany can witness, yea,
all the world, for which Faustus hath lost both Germany
and the world, yea, heaven itself – heaven, the seat of
God, the throne of the blessed, the kingdom of joy – and   50
must remain in hell for ever. Hell, ah, hell for ever! Sweet
friends, what shall become of Faustus, being in hell for
ever?

3 SCH. Yet, Faustus, call on God.

FAU. On God, whom Faustus hath abjured? on God, whom
Faustus hath blasphemed? Ah, my God, I would weep,
but the devil draws in my tears. Gush forth blood, instead
of tears, yea, life and soul! O, he stays my tongue! I would
lift up my hands, but see, they hold them, they hold them.

ALL. Who, Faustus?   60

FAU. Why, Lucifer and Mephostophilis. Ah, gentlemen, I
gave them my soul for my cunning.

ALL. God forbid!

FAU. God forbade it, indeed; but Faustus hath done it. For
the vain pleasure of four-and-twenty years hath Faustus
lost eternal joy and felicity. I writ them a bill with mine

62. *cunning:* skill.
66. *bill:* deed.

NOTES: p. 177

own blood: the date is expired, this is the time, and he wiil
fetch me.

1 SCH. Why did not Faustus tell us of this before, that divines
might have prayed for thee?   70

FAU. Oft have I thought to have done so; but the devil threatened to tear me in pieces if I named God, to fetch me body
and soul if I once gave ear to divinity; and now 'tis too
late. Gentlemen, away, lest you perish with me!

2 SCH. O, what may we do to save Faustus?

FAU. Talk not of me, but save yourselves and depart.

3 SCH. God will strengthen me. I will stay with Faustus.

1 SCH. Tempt not God, sweet friend; but let us into the next
room and there pray for him.

FAU. Ay, pray for me, pray for me; and, what noise soever ye   80
hear, come not unto me, for nothing can rescue me.

2 SCH. Pray thou, and we will pray, that God may have mercy
upon thee.

FAU. Gentlemen, farewell. If I live till morning, I'll visit you;
if not, Faustus is gone to hell.

ALL. Faustus, farewell.   *Exeunt* Scholars.

MEPH. Ay, Faustus, now thou hast no hope of heaven;
Therefore despair, think only upon hell,
For that must be thy mansion, there to dwell.

FAU. O thou bewitching fiend, 'twas thy temptation   90
Hath robb'd me of eternal happiness.

MEPH. I do confess it, Faustus, and rejoice.
'Twas I that, when thou wert i' the way to heaven,
Damm'd up thy passage; when thou took'st the book
To view the scriptures, then I turn'd the leaves
And led thine eye.
What, weep'st thou? 'tis too late, despair, farewell!
Fools that will laugh on earth must weep in hell.   *Exit.*

Enter the Good Angel *and the* Bad Angel *at several doors.*

GOOD ANG. O Faustus, if thou hadst given ear to me,

78. *let us:* let us go.
91. *Hath:* which hath.

NOTES: p. 177

Innumerable joys had follow'd thee;   100
But thou didst love the world.

BAD ANG.   Gave ear to me,
And now must taste hell's pains perpetually.

GOOD ANG. O, what will all thy riches, pleasures, pomps
Avail thee now?

BAD ANG.   Nothing but vex thee more,
To want in hell, that had on earth such store.

Music while the throne descends.

GOOD ANG. O, thou hast lost celestial happiness,
Pleasures unspeakable, bliss without end.
Hadst thou affected sweet divinity,
Hell or the devil had had no power on thee.
Hadst thou kept on that way, Faustus, behold   110
In what resplendent glory thou hadst sit
In yonder throne, like those bright shining saints,
And triumph'd over hell; that hast thou lost.
And now, poor soul, must thy good angel leave thee;
The jaws of hell are open to receive thee.   *Exit.*

Hell is discovered.

BAD ANG. Now, Faustus, let thine eyes with horror stare
Into that vast perpetual torture-house.
There are the furies, tossing damned souls
On burning forks; their bodies boil in lead:
There are live quarters broiling on the coals,   120
That ne'er can die: this ever-burning chair
Is for o'er-tortur'd souls to rest them in:
These that are fed with sops of flaming fire
Were gluttons and lov'd only delicates
And laugh'd to see the poor starve at their gates.
But yet all these are nothing; thou shalt see
Ten thousand tortures that more horrid be.

FAU. O, I have seen enough to torture me.

BAD ANG. Nay, thou must feel them, taste the smart of all:

105. *store:* plenty.
108. *affected:* been drawn to, preferred.
124. *delicates:* delicacies.

NOTES: p. 177

He that loves pleasure must for pleasure fall: 130
And so I leave thee, Faustus, till anon;
Then wilt thou tumble in confusion.   *Exit.*
                              The clock strikes eleven.

FAU. Ah, Faustus,
Now hast thou but one bare hour to live,
And then thou must be damn'd perpetually.
Stand still, you ever-moving spheres of heaven,
That time may cease, and midnight never come;
Fair nature's eye, rise, rise again, and make
Perpetual day; or let this hour be but
A year, a month, a week, a natural day,   140
That Faustus may repent and save his soul.
O lente lente currite noctis equi !
The stars move still, time runs, the clock will strike,
The devil will come, and Faustus must be damn'd.
O, I'll leap up to my God! Who pulls me down?
See, see where Christ's blood streams in the firmament!
One drop would save my soul, half a drop. Ah, my Christ! –
Rend not my heart for naming of my Christ;
Yet will I call on him. O, spare me, Lucifer! –
Where is it now? 'Tis gone: and see where God   150
Stretcheth out his arm and bends his ireful brows.
Mountains and hills, come, come, and fall on me,
And hide me from the heavy wrath of God!
No, no:
Then will I headlong run into the earth.
Earth, gape! O, no, it will not harbour me.
You stars that reign'd at my nativity,
Whose influence hath allotted death and hell,
Now draw up Faustus like a foggy mist
Into the entrails of yon labouring cloud,   160

131. *till anon:* until by and by.
138. *nature's eye:* sun.
140. *a natural day:* a mere day.
143. *still:* unceasingly.
160. *labouring:* heavy, stormy.

NOTES: pp. 177–8

That, when you vomit forth into the air,
My limbs may issue from your smoky mouths,
So that my soul may but ascend to heaven.   *The watch strikes.*
Ah, half the hour is pass'd: 'twill all be pass'd anon.
O God,
If thou wilt not have mercy on my soul,
Yet for Christ's sake, whose blood hath ransom'd me,
Impose some end to my incessant pain;
Let Faustus live in hell a thousand years,
A hundred thousand, and at last be sav'd.   170
O, no end is limited to damned souls.
Why wert thou not a creature wanting soul?
Or why is this immortal that thou hast?
Ah, Pythagoras' *metempsychosis*, were that true,
This soul should fly from me and I be chang'd
Unto some brutish beast: all beasts are happy,
For when they die
Their souls are soon dissolv'd in elements;
But mine must live still to be plagu'd in hell.
Curs'd be the parents that engender'd me!   180
No, Faustus, curse thyself, curse Lucifer
That hath depriv'd thee of the joys of heaven.
                              The clock striketh twelve.
O, it strikes, it strikes! Now, body, turn to air,
Or Lucifer will bear thee quick to hell!
                              Thunder and lightning.
O soul, be chang'd into little water drops,
And fall into the ocean, ne'er be found.

                    Enter Devils.

My God, my God! Look not so fierce on me!
Adders and serpents, let me breathe awhile!

163. Stage-direction: *watch:* clock.
171. *limited:* appointed, fixed definitely.
176. *Unto:* into, to.
179. *still:* ever.
184. *quick:* alive.

NOTES: p. 179

Ugly hell, gape not! Come not, Lucifer;
I'll burn my books! – Ah, Mephostophilis!   190
Exeunt with him. [*Exeunt* LUCIFER *and* BEELZEBUB.]

Scene XX

Enter the Scholars.

1 SCH. Come, gentlemen, let us go visit Faustus,
    For such a dreadful night was never seen
    Since first the world's creation did begin;
    Such fearful shrieks and cries were never heard.
    Pray heaven the doctor have escap'd the danger.
2 SCH. O, help us, heaven! see, here are Faustus' limbs,
    All torn asunder by the hand of death.
3 SCH. The devils whom Faustus serv'd have torn him thus;
    For, 'twixt the hours of twelve and one, methought
    I heard him shriek and call aloud for help,   10
    At which self time the house seem'd all on fire
    With dreadful horror of these damned fiends.
2 SCH. Well, gentlemen, though Faustus' end be such
    As every Christian heart laments to think on,
    Yet, for he was a scholar, once admir'd
    For wondrous knowledge in our German schools,
    We'll give his mangled limbs due burial;
    And all the students, cloth'd in mourning black,
    Shall wait upon his heavy funeral.   *Exeunt.*

> 19. *wait upon:* accompany on its way.
> *heavy:* sad, sorrowful.

NOTES: p. 179

Epilogue

Enter Chorus.

CHO. Cut is the branch that might have grown full straight,
And burned is Apollo's laurel bough
That sometime grew within this learned man.
Faustus is gone: regard his hellish fall,
Whose fiendful fortune may exhort the wise
Only to wonder at unlawful things,
Whose deepness doth entice such forward wits
To practise more than heavenly power permits.   [*Exit.*]

Terminat hora diem; terminat Author opus.

FINIS.

3. *sometime:* at one time.
5. *fiendful:* proceeding from diabolical agency.
7. *forward wits:* advanced thinkers.

NOTES: p. 179

Notes

DOCTOR FAUSTUS

DRAMATIS PERSONAE

8 *Pope Adrian:* An imaginary character, though a Pope Adrian VI did reign very briefly during the lifetime of the historical Faustus. The playwright modelled his pope in part on the twelfth-century Alexander III. See note on viii, 90–6.

9–10 Raymond and Bruno seem to have had no historical originals.

13 *Charles V, Emperor of Germany:* He ruled from 1519 until his retirement in 1556, that is, for a period which included the last twenty years or so of the life of the historical Faustus.

27–8 *Good Angel. / Bad Angel:* Marlowe added these morality-play characters to the story of Faustus as he found it in the *Damnable Life.*

29 *Mephostophilis:* The edition of 1616 favours this spelling of the name; the playwrights' source-book, the *Damnable Life*, uses the similar form 'Mephostophiles'.

32–8 *the Seven Deadly Sins:* Often personified in mediaeval literature: for example, in *Piers Plowman*, V, and in morality plays. During Marlowe's lifetime, they made a well-known appearance in Spenser's *Faerie Queene*, I, iv.

39 *Alexander the Great:* King of Macedon (356–323 B.C.); the most famous of all the conquerors of the ancient world.

40 *His Paramour:* Thais, an Athenian courtesan. See Dryden's *Alexander's Feast.*

41 *Darius, King of Persia:* He spent most of his short reign defending his empire against Alexander the Great. After his defeat, one of his subordinates murdered him (331 B.C.).

42 *Helen:* Paris seduced her and carried her off to Troy. Her husband Menelaus, King of Sparta, and the other Greek princes fought the Trojan War to get her back. Poets in many ages, down to W. B. Yeats in the present century, have thought of Helen of Troy as the type of female beauty.

149

PROLOGUE

1–6 These lines refer to three previous plays, from which *Doctor Faustus* is to differ markedly. The first of them evidently dramatized the Carthaginian defeat of the Romans at Lake Trasimene in central Italy in 217 B.C. There is no other trace of it. If the other two were plays by Marlowe himself, and not merely plays recently performed by the company for which he was writing, *Edward II* could have been the play presenting 'the dalliance of love / In courts of kings where state is overturn'd', and *Tamburlaine* could have been the play concerned with 'the pomp of proud audacious deeds'.

2 *Mars:* The god of war.

12 *Rhode:* Roda (since 1922, Stadtroda) in central Germany.

13 *Wittenberg:* Like Luther and Hamlet, Faustus was a member of the university which had been founded in this East German town in 1502.

16 *The fruitful plot of scholarism grac'd:* 'The fruitful garden of scholarship being adorned by him'.

17 *grac'd with doctor's name:* Marlowe alludes punningly to the Cambridge official 'grace' permitting a candidate to get his degree. This kind of play on words is typical of him. Compare 'perform / The form' nine lines earlier; and 'Whose termine is term'd the world's wide pole' (vi, 42).

20 *cunning of a self-conceit:* 'intellectual pride engendered by arrogance'.

21 *waxen wings:* Marlowe refers to the death of Icarus, who flew too close to the sun, with the result that it melted the wax attaching his wings to his body and he fell into the sea.

22 *melting:* i.e., the wings melting.

27 *before his chiefest bliss:* 'to his hopes of salvation'.

SCENE 1

Stage-direction: *Faustus in his study:* The Chorus, before leaving the stage, draws aside a curtain and reveals Faustus. Faustus evidently has a number of large volumes by him, and, as he reviews and in turn rejects the permissible studies of philosophy, medicine, law, and divinity, he picks up, quotes from, and lays down one after another of these.

3 *commenc'd:* Like 'grac'd', 'commenc'd' is a technical Cambridge term.

4 *level at the end of every art:* 'aim at that which all arts try to do'.

5–7 At this date, the university curriculum was still dominated by the writings of the great Greek philosopher Aristotle (384–322 B.C.); but his supremacy had recently been challenged by the intellectual reformer and opponent of scholasticism Petrus Ramus (Pierre de la Ramée, 1515–72). While Marlowe was at Cambridge, William Temple was successfully defending Ramism against the attacks of Everard Digby. Marlowe's play *The Massacre at Paris*, vi, testifies to its author's knowledge of Ramus' theories and of his violent death; and the Latin definition of the purpose of logic in the present passage, 'To argue well is the end of logic', derives not from Aristotle, as Faustus implies, but from Ramus.

6 *Analytics:* Aristotle's *Prior Analytics* and *Posterior Analytics*, works on the nature of proof in argument.

12 *on kai me on:* A transliteration of the Greek phrase meaning 'being and not being'.
Galen: A second-century Greek physician and prolific author, who was accepted throughout the Middle Ages as the leading authority on medical science.

13 *ubi desinit philosophus, ibi incipit medicus:* 'Where the philosopher leaves off, there the physician begins.' The sentence is freely adapted from Aristotle.

16 *Summum bonum medicinae sanitas:* 'The greatest good of medicine is health.' Another quotation from Aristotle.

20 *bills hung up as monuments:* 'prescriptions displayed as enduring examples of medical art'.

27 *Justinian:* The sixth-century emperor of Constantinople who codified the Roman law.

28–9, 31 Faustus quotes loosely from the *Institutes* of Justinian. The first quotation means, 'If one and the same thing is bequeathed to two persons, one of them shall have the thing, the other the value of the thing, etc.'; the second quotation means, 'A father cannot disinherit his son, except – '.

38 *Jerome's Bible:* The Vulgate, or Latin translation of the Bible prepared mainly by St Jerome.

39 *Stipendium peccati mors est:* Faustus' quotation breaks off misleadingly. The Authorized Version renders the whole sentence

as follows: 'For the wages of sin is death; but the gift of God is eternal life through Jesus Christ our Lord' (Rom. vi, 23).

40–1 *Si peccasse negamus, fallimur, et nulla est in nobis veritas:* Faustus quotes, and then translates, 1 John i, 8.

43–4 *and so consequently die:* There is nothing subversive of Christian doctrine in a demonstration that man is condemned by the letter of the law. What is unorthodox is Faustus' refusal to see that man, thus condemned, may be redeemed by the sacrifice of Christ. See Rom. vi, 23, quoted above.

46 *Che sarà, sarà:* An Italian proverb, immediately translated by Faustus.

50 *Lines, circles, letters, and characters:* Magicians were accustomed to draw 'lines' and 'circles' around themselves for protection against evil spirits; they made use of magical combinations of 'letters' taken from the several forms of the divine name; and they employed as charms the 'characters' or signs appropriated to good spirits of various kinds.

55 *quiet poles:* The celestial spheres were believed to revolve on a common axle-tree which was itself motionless. Being motionless, its poles were 'quiet'.

59 *his dominion that exceeds in this:* 'the dominion of him who excels in this art'.

68 Stage-direction: *Enter the Angel and Spirit:* i.e., the Good Angel and the Bad Angel. In *Doctor Faustus*, 'spirit' invariably means an evil spirit or devil. It is reasonable to assume that the angels enter by separate doors and that each of them uses the same door throughout the play. See the stage-direction after xix, 98.

72 *that:* i.e., the book of magic.

75 *Jove:* Marlowe was not alone in the Renaissance period in occasionally applying to the God of Christianity the name of the greatest of the Roman gods. He does it twice more in *Doctor Faustus*: in iii, 91, and in Cho. 1, 3.

77 *glutted with conceit of this:* 'filled with the notion of obtaining such power'.

81 *India:* In Marlowe's time, the name could refer to either the East or the West Indies. It probably means the East Indies here in contrast to the 'new-found' America two lines later.

87 *I'll have them wall all Germany with brass:* The second scene of
Robert Greene's comedy *Friar Bacon and Friar Bungay* shows
Roger Bacon planning to wall England with brass.

88 *swift Rhine:* instead of the Elbe, on which Wittenberg stands.

89–90 *silk / Wherewith the students shall be bravely clad:* The univer-
sities required students to dress plainly.

92 *the Prince of Parma:* Spanish governor-general of the Netherlands, then nominally part of the Empire, from 1579 until his
death in 1592. He was the foremost soldier of his time. In 1588
the Spanish Armada was to have enabled him to invade England.

95 *the fiery keel at Antwerp's bridge:* On 4 April 1585, a fireship dis-
patched by the Netherlanders shattered the bridge which Parma
had built over the Scheldt to complete the blockade of Antwerp.
Though Parma's prompt energy enabled him to restore the situation, the Spaniards did not forget this 'hell-burner', and the re-
collection of it augmented the effect upon them of the English
fireships off Calais in 1588.

103 *will receive no object:* Different editors have explained this phrase
in different ways. The general sense is clearly 'will think of nothing else'. Since philosophy, medicine, jurisprudence, and theology were sometimes called the 'objective' disciplines, the phrase
may mean 'will not receive anything offered in the ordinary (academic) way'. Other suggested paraphrases include 'will admit no
obstacle' and 'will not be impressed by solid realities'.

107 *basest of the three:* 'even baser than the other three'.

114–15 *as the infernal spirits / On sweet Musaeus when he came to hell:*
Musaeus, the legendary pre-Homeric Greek poet and pupil of
Orpheus, is glimpsed standing head and shoulders above the
spirits who throng around him in the underworld in Virgil's
Aeneid, vi, 666–7. Marlowe may have had this passage in mind.
Alternatively, he may have confused Musaeus with Orpheus, who
followed his dead wife Eurydice into the underworld in the hope
of winning her back and there charmed the infernal spirits with
his music.

116–17 *Agrippa . . . / Whose shadows made all Europe honour him:*
Henry Cornelius Agrippa von Nettesheim (1486–1535), humanist and reputed magician, was credited with the power of calling
up the 'shadows' of the dead.

119 *canonize:* 'enrol among famous persons'. Accented on the second syllable.

120 *Moors:* At this time, used generally of members of dark-coloured races. Here, the natives of the Spanish possessions in America.

124 *Like Almain rutters with their horsemen's staves:* 'Like German cavalrymen with their lances'.

125 *Lapland giants:* Marlowe has an earlier allusion to these mythical Arctic giants near the beginning of the second part of *Tamburlaine,* where he speaks of Greenland as 'Inhabited with tall and sturdy men, / Giants as big as hugy Polypheme'.

128 *queen of love:* Venus.

130 *golden fleece:* Gold from the American mines carried to Spain in the annual plate-fleet. By calling it 'the golden fleece', Marlowe compares it with the treasure brought back from Colchis by Jason and the Argonauts. It is possible that the word 'argosies' (l. 129), which was often wrongly supposed to be derived from the name of Jason's ship, the *Argo,* suggested this image to him. In fact, an argosy was originally a ship out of the port of Ragusa (now known as Dubrovnik).

131 *old Philip:* Only son of the Emperor Charles V, he became King of Spain on his father's retirement and reigned until 1598. Since Faustus is later to perform before the Emperor Charles V, this reference to Philip II, like the earlier reference to the Prince of Parma, is anachronistic. But *Doctor Faustus* resembles other plays of its time in being the product of impetuous genius rather than of critical scholarship.

134 *object it not:* 'do not bring it forward as a condition that I should be resolute'.

138 *tongues:* Especially Latin, the language in which it was believed spirits had to be addressed. Also Greek and Hebrew.
well seen in minerals: 'well-versed in the properties of minerals'.

142 *Delphian oracle:* The oracle of Apollo at Delphi on the slope of Mount Parnassus was the most famous oracle of the ancient world.

153 *Bacon:* Roger Bacon (1214?–94) was an early English scientist and a reputed magician.
Abanus: Pietro d'Abano (1250?–1316?) was an Italian physician and philosopher and a suspected sorcerer.

154 *The Hebrew Psalter, and New Testament:* The Psalms and the
opening verses of the Gospel of St John were regularly used in
conjurations.

157 *the words of art:* with which to conjure, or call up spirits.

SCENE ii

2 *sic probo:* 'I prove it thus.' Used in scholastic disputations.

7 *follows not:* 'is not a logical consequence'. Wagner facetiously addresses the Scholars with the formal precision of scholastic argument. He insists first that it does not follow, from the fact that
God knows, that he, Wagner, knows (ll. 5–7); and then that it
does not follow, from the fact that he knows, that he will tell
them (ll. 8–12).

10 *licentiates:* 'holders of an initial degree admitting you to candidacy
for a master's or doctor's degree'.

14–15 *is he not corpus naturale? and is not that mobile?* 'is he not a
natural body? and is not a natural body liable to move?' The
current scholastic expression for the subject-matter of physics
was 'corpus naturale seu mobile', meaning 'a body that is natural
or liable to move'. It is an adaptation of an expression of Aristotle's.

19 *the place of execution:* i.e., the dining-room. But Wagner immediately exploits the phrase in its more usual sense by saying that
he expects to see his hearers hanged.

20–6 His parody of scholastic argument having enabled him to triumph over his listeners, Wagner assumes an appropriate facial
expression and proceeds to a parody of Puritan unctuousness.

24 *this wine:* carried by Wagner.

30 *ally'd to me:* in friendship.

SCENE iii

Stage-direction: *Lucifer and four Devils above:* Witnesses of what
Faustus does, but unseen by him, they presumably stand upon
the balcony or upper stage.

1–4 Marlowe may here have been echoing Spenser's *Faerie Queene*,
III, x, 46: 'Now gan the humid vapour shed the ground / With
perly deaw, and th' Earthes gloomy shade / Did dim the bright-
nesse of the welkin round'.

2 *Orion's drizzling look:* There are references to the rainy constella-
tion of Orion in Virgil's *Aeneid*, i, 535, and iv, 52.

3 *from th' antarctic world:* Marlowe must have supposed, at least
while writing these lines, that the night advanced from the southern hemisphere!

9 *anagrammatiz'd:* Conjurors seeking to call up spirits commonly
used anagrams of the mystic Hebrew name of God. An anagram
is a word or phrase formed by transposing letters from some
other word or phrase.

12 *characters of signs and erring stars:* 'symbols of the signs of the
Zodiac and the planets'.

14 *to be resolute:* When Valdes in i, 132 appeared to doubt whether
Faustus would be resolute, Faustus told him to silence his doubt.
Nevertheless, he now has to exhort himself to be resolute in his
conjuration.

16–24 'May the gods of Acheron be favourable to me! Away with
the threefold spirit of Jehovah! Hail, spirits of fire, air, water,
and earth! Lucifer prince of the east, Beelzebub monarch of burning hell, and Demogorgon, we ask your favour that Mephostophilis may appear and rise! . . . Why do you delay? By Jehovah,
hell, and the holy water which I now sprinkle, and by the sign
of the cross which I now make, and by our prayers, may Mephostophilis himself now rise, compelled to our service!'

16 *Acherontis:* Acheron, one of the rivers of Hades, stands here for
Hades itself.

16–17 *numen triplex Iehovae:* By 'the threefold spirit of Jehovah'
Faustus means the Trinity. In the lines that follow, he turns to
the infernal trinity of Lucifer, Beelzebub, and Demogorgon.

20 Stage-direction: *Dragon appears briefly above:* The goods belonging to the Admiral's men in 1598 included '1 dragon in *Faustus*'.
Presumably this was made to appear on the upper stage to represent the dragon that, according to the *Damnable Life*, 'hanged
hovering in the air' over Faustus.

21 *Quid tu moraris?* Believing that the spirits would be reluctant to
appear, magicians commonly inserted such phrases as this into
their spells.

24 Stage-direction: *a Devil:* Mephostophilis.

36 *Quin redis, Mephostophilis, fratris imagine!* 'Why don't you return, Mephostophilis, in the likeness of a friar!'

48 *That was the cause, but yet per accidens:* 'Your conjuring was the cause, not because of what it was in itself, but because of something it happened to include.' 'Per accidens' is another scholastic expression.

57-8 *So Faustus hath | Already done:* by abjuring the Trinity in ll. 16–17.

62 *confounds hell in Elysium:* 'does not distinguish between hell and Elysium'.

63 *the old philosophers:* Faustus feels akin to them in spirit because they share his disbelief in an eternity of punishment or reward. He is quoting a saying attributed to Averroes (1126–98), an Arab medical writer and commentator upon Aristotle.

70 *aspiring:* Mephostophilis uses this word to describe the sin by which Lucifer fell; his predecessor Tamburlaine declared that 'Nature . . . / Doth teach us all to have aspiring minds' (1 *Tamburlaine*, II, vii, 18–20). From the beginning of his career as a playwright, Marlowe seems to have thought that it was in human nature to aspire; when he came to write *Doctor Faustus* he still thought so but believed that a terrible price would have to be paid for yielding to the impulse. The word 'aspiring' refers to one of the dominant themes in his work.

76–7 The metrical incompleteness of l. 76 ensures that a pause follows it, while Faustus collects himself, after the blunt 'In hell', to ask argumentatively, 'How come it then that thou art out of hell?'

78 *Why, this is hell, nor am I out of it:* Milton's Satan testifies similarly, 'Which way I fly is Hell; myself am Hell' (*Paradise Lost*, iv, 75).

79–82 Mephostophilis is quoting St John Chrysostom, the fourth-century Greek Father, who states that ten thousand hells are as nothing in comparison with the loss of celestial bliss.

87 *manly:* By using this word, Faustus expresses the sense of human self-sufficiency which he enjoys at this stage in his career. For the reader or listener, there is irony in his arrogant recommendation of manliness to a supernatural being.

91 *Jove's deity:* God. See note on i, 75.

104–16 Faustus can hardly contain his eagerness to conclude the compact. Mephostophilis, when they next meet, will exhibit an equal eagerness to secure his soul (v, 73, 82).

109–10 Faustus plans to unite Spain with Africa at the Straits of Gibraltar.

SCENE iv

3–4 *You have seen many boys with such pickedevants, I am sure:*
Uttered with indignant sarcasm.

5 *comings in:* 'earnings'. The phrase gives Robin an opportunity of
punning on 'goings out' (l. 6), by which he means (i) 'expenses'
and (ii) 'parts of my body protruding through my tattered
clothes'. Wagner alludes to Robin's 'nakedness' in l. 7.

9–10 *he would give his soul to the devil for a shoulder of mutton:* A
ludicrous echo of the main theme, such as may be found in the
comic scenes of other plays of the period. But Robin begins by
being more prudent than Faustus; in ll. 11–12 he says that he
would demand a higher price for his soul than Wagner supposes.

14 *Qui mihi discipulus:* 'You who are my pupil'. These are the open-
ing words of a didactic poem, *Carmen de Moribus*, by William
Lily (1466?–1522) the schoolmaster, which was much read in
Elizabethan grammar-schools.

16 *beaten silk:* 'embroidered silk'. But Wagner is punning and means
also that he will thrash Robin.

20 *bind thyself:* as a servant.

23–4 *they are as familiar with me as if they paid for their meat and
drink:* 'they treat me with as little ceremony as if they were guests
who had paid for their dinner and I the waiter whose business it
was to serve them (with my own flesh and blood)'.

26 *take these guilders:* 'take these Dutch florins as hiring-money'.

27 *marry:* An exclamation, here of surprise, derived from the name
of the Virgin Mary.

47–8 *quasi vestigiis nostris insistere:* 'tread as it were in our footsteps'.

SCENE v

Stage-direction: *in his study:* Faustus is again revealed by the drawing back of a curtain.

6–7 As previously in iii, 14, Faustus exhorts himself to 'be resolute'.
He wavers, however, and his irresolution is reflected in the
rhythm of these two alexandrines. The play contains many lines
longer, and many shorter, than the standard pentameter, and such
lines are often used as expressively as here.

15 *Go forward, Faustus, in that famous art:* This line exactly repeats i, 73.

17 *what of these?* i.e., how can these help me now?

24 *Emden:* This port in north-west Germany was in the sixteenth century the headquarters of Europe's largest merchant fleet. It had trade relations with England.

30 *Veni, veni, Mephostophilis!* 'Come, come, Mephostophilis!'

42 *Solamen miseris socios habuisse doloris:* 'To the unhappy, it is a comfort to have had companions in misfortune.' This Latin hexameter seems not to be of classical origin. A number of writers quote it, but its author is unknown.

48 *him:* i.e., Lucifer. Mephostophilis is merely his agent.

61–3 The *Damnable Life* says nothing about the congealing of Faustus' blood and the bringing of fire.

63, 70 *fire:* A disyllable.

68 *is not thy soul thy own?* Faustus' rhetorical question expresses again his sense of human self-sufficiency. Compare iii, 87.

70 *set it on:* i.e., put the saucer of blood on the chafer.

73, 82 The eagerness of Mephostophilis here matches that of Faustus in iii, 104–16.

74 *Consummatum est:* 'It is finished.' See John xix, 30. Marlowe daringly places in Faustus' mouth the last words of Christ on the cross.

77, 81 *Homo fuge!* 'Fly, O man!'

86–9 Faustus' decision to ignore the warnings and hand over the deed is highlighted by its embodiment in these rhyming couplets.

120–7 Mephostophilis declares first of all that hell exists at the centre of the sublunary, elemental part of the universe. He then goes on to explain that hell is not merely a particular place but a condition: 'where we are is hell' (l. 123). He has already spoken to this effect in iii, 78, 'Why, this is hell, nor am I out of it.' There is nothing like this in the *Damnable Life*.

125–6 *when all the world dissolves / And every creature shall be purify'd:* i.e., at Doomsday, when the whole world is destroyed by fire, and every created thing is no longer mixed, but of one essence, either wholly good or wholly evil.

127 *is:* Marlowe presumably regarded the subject 'All places' as singular in thought, that is, as equivalent to 'every place'.

156 *Penelope:* The faithful wife of Ulysses, who successfully baffled her importunate suitors during her husband's long absence.

157 *Saba:* The Queen of Sheba. See 1 Kings x.

162 *lightning:* A trisyllable.

169 Stage-direction: *There turn to them:* Mephostophilis shows Faustus that the instructions he seeks are to be found in the book already given to him. The process is repeated at ll. 173 and 179.

179 *warrant thee:* i.e., assure you that the book contains all that I say.

SCENE vi

Stage-direction: *in his study:* For the third time, Faustus is 'discovered' at the beginning of a scene.

5–7 To encourage Faustus not to repent of his bargain, Mephostophilis extols the 'manly' values which Faustus himself upheld in iii, 87 and v, 68.

20 *thunders:* The third person plural in -s is not uncommon in Elizabethan English. Compare viii, 12 and xviii, 125–6.

21–3 This prepares for the dramatized temptation to suicide at xviii, 56.

27 *Alexander:* Paris, the lover of Oenone, is usually so named by 'blind Homer' in the *Iliad*. He deserted Oenone for Helen. After his death, Oenone took her own life. See Tennyson's *Oenone* and *The Death of Oenone*.

28–9 Amphion played with such skill that the stones moved of their own accord to form the walls of Thebes.

32 *I am resolv'd:* As at the beginning of scene v, loss of hope leads Faustus to a renewed determination to 'be resolute' in his devotion to the powers he has invoked.

35–61 According to the view of the universe that was current when Marlowe wrote, the earth is enclosed within a series of concentric crystal 'spheres' (ll. 35, 40, 59), to which the sun, moon, planets, and stars are fixed, and by which they are carried around the stationary earth. Marlowe evidently recognized 'nine' (l. 60) of these spheres or 'heavens' (ll. 38, 59), the first eight of them being in motion. The nearest is the sphere of the moon (ll. 35, 39), within which all is subject to decay. Beyond it, where all is eternal, are the spheres of the six other 'erring stars' (l. 44) or 'planets' (l. 51), all seven of which, including the sun, are named in ll. 53–5.

The 'firmament' (l. 60), or sphere of the fixed stars, then completes the visible universe. Outside all eight of these, there is the immovable 'empyreal heaven' (ll. 60–1) or 'empyreal orb' (l. 39), which is the abode of God.

36–44 Faustus wishes to know whether the entire universe is spherical as is the earth at the centre of it. Mephostophilis tells him that it is, explaining that just as in the sublunary, elemental part of the universe the element of fire encloses that of air, which in turn encloses the elements of water and earth, so in the celestial part each sphere is enclosed by the sphere which is beyond it, the moving spheres having all a single axle-tree. Since Saturn, Mars, Jupiter, and the rest have their separate planetary spheres within the 'empyreal orb', it is not wrong, he concludes, to give them individual names.

45 *both situ et tempore:* 'both in position and in time'. The sentence as a whole means, 'But do they all move in the same direction and revolve round the earth in the same time?'

46–8 The planets appear to travel daily right round the earth from east to west; each one of them also seems, while doing this, to be travelling at its own, much slower, pace in another direction. This slower apparent motion determines the changing times of rising and setting.

48 *the poles of the zodiac:* i.e., the common axle-tree on which all the spheres revolve.

53–5 *Saturn . . . days:* These figures are approximately correct, with one exception: that for Mars is about twice what it should be.

56 *suppositions:* In scholastic logic, a supposition is something held to be true and taken as the basis of an argument.

57 *dominion or intelligentia:* It was believed that angels or intelligences directed the turning of the celestial spheres. The notion is Platonic.

62–3 The *coelum crystallinum*, or crystalline sphere, was a tenth celestial sphere which had been introduced into astronomical theory to account for the 'trepidation of the spheres' (Donne, *A Valediction: forbidding mourning*), that is, the supposed variation in the rate of precession of the equinoxes. Some thinkers held that there was also a *coelum igneum*, or fiery sphere; but Mephostophilis was not alone in denying its existence. In restricting himself to eight moving spheres, he was in line with certain

sceptical, empirical Renaissance writers on astronomy, who refused to believe in moving spheres unfurnished with visible
bodies by which their motions could be directly observed.

65 *conjunctions, oppositions, aspects, eclipses:* A conjunction is an apparent proximity to each other of two heavenly bodies. An oppo-
sition is an extreme apparent divergence. These and certain other
relative positions are called aspects. Astrologers ascribe special
significance to the various aspects and to eclipses.

68 *Per inaequalem motum respectu totius:* 'On account of their un-
equal motion with respect to the whole.' Mephostophilis means
that the heavenly bodies do not all have the same speed and direction of movement.

74 *against our kingdom:* i.e., contrary to the interests of the infernal
monarchy.

77 *this:* i.e., my previous speech.

86 *Help to save distressed Faustus' soul:* A pointed echo of l. 79.

94 *contrary:* Accented on the second syllable.

96 *dam:* 'mother'. The phrase 'the devil and his dam' was a common
Elizabethan tag.

105 *pastime:* In the *Damnable Life*, this does not take the form of a
show of the Seven Deadly Sins. See 'Introduction'. Some critics
have taken a dislike to the show. But its grotesque humour effectively concludes the four scenes, i, iii, v, and vi, which show
Faustus' commitment of himself to evil. After it, Faustus sets
about exploiting such powers as he has gained.

110 *Talk not of paradise or creation:* Such talk would be 'against our
kingdom' (l. 74).

115 *Pride:* At the head of the seven comes the chief sin, the sin by
which Lucifer fell and to which Faustus has succumbed.

116 *Ovid's flea:* In an *Elegia de Pulice*, a Latin poem of uncertain
date which was at one time wrongly ascribed to Ovid, the poet
envies the flea for its ability – in the words of the play – to 'creep
into every corner of a wench'.

122 *cloth of arras:* To cover a floor with this rich tapestry fabric, as
Pride demands, would be extravagantly ostentatious.

130–1 *begotten of a chimney-sweeper and an oyster-wife:* therefore
black and stinking.

143 *some of you shall be:* 'one of you is sure to prove'.

151 *Martlemas-beef:* Salt beef hung up on St Martin's day, 11 November, this being the customary time for the annual slaughter of cattle for salting and winter consumption.

154 *March-beer:* A strong beer brewed in March.

160, 163 *Heigh-ho!* This exclamation expresses the yawning of Sloth.

167 *mutton:* A cant term for a prostitute.

167–8 *the first letter of my name begins with Lechery:* This was a well-known facetious form of words. Another example of it occurs in John Lyly's *Euphues and his England*: 'There is not far hence a gentlewoman whom I have long time loved . . . the first letter of whose name . . . is Camilla'.

180 Stage-direction: *Exeunt omnes several ways:* 'All depart, in different directions.' Presumably Faustus and Mephostophilis go one way, Lucifer and Beelzebub another.

SCENE vii

1 *look to the horses:* Robin has found employment as an ostler at an inn. Wishing to experiment with the book of magic which he has stolen from Faustus, he tries to get his fellow-ostler, Dick, to take over his work.

7 *A per se, a; t, h, e, the; o per se, o:* Robin is reading from the book with difficulty. He means, 'A, by itself, spells a; t, h, e, spells the; o, by itself, spells o.'

7–8 *deny orgon, gorgon:* Robin is evidently struggling to read the name 'Demogorgon', which has already figured in Faustus' invocation at iii, 19.

12 *circle:* i.e., magician's circle drawn for protection against evil spirits.

15 *he'll conjure you:* 'he'll give it you!'

19 *my mistress hath done it:* i.e., his wife has already given him horns by cuckolding him. There was an old and widespread belief that a wife's infidelity could produce this result.

20–1 *waded as deep into matters as other men:* A *double entendre*. Robin is suggesting that he has been the lover of their mistress. For the equivocal use of 'matters', compare Shakespeare's *Julius Caesar*, I, i: 'I meddle with no tradesman's matters, nor women's matters'.

27 *to the tavern:* from which they emerge at the beginning of scene x.

29 *whippincrust:* A humorous distortion of 'hippocras'. This was a cordial drink, made of wine flavoured with spices, which had been named after Hippocrates, the 'Father of Medicine'. The word 'whippincrust' possibly contains a suggestion of 'whipping-cheer', i.e., flogging.

31–2 *as dry as a dog:* A current proverbial saying.

CHORUS I

The scenes showing Faustus' exploitation of his dearly-bought power are aptly prefaced by this narrative account of such of his travels as cannot easily be put on the stage.

3 *Jove:* God. See note on i, 75.

4 *Olympus:* The lofty mountain that was regarded in Greek mythology as the home of the gods.

8 *The tropics, zones, and quarters of the sky:* i.e. the tropics of Cancer and Capricorn, and the five zones in which they and the polar circles divide or 'quarter' the heavens.

9–10 'From the lowest to the highest of the moving spheres'. The *primum mobile*, i.e., 'the first moving thing', was a sphere which imparted motion to each sphere or 'circle' that it enclosed. Marlowe, acknowledging only nine spheres altogether, identifies the *primum mobile* with the firmament, or sphere of the fixed stars.

11 *this circumference:* beyond which lay only the empyrean. In other words, Faustus was able to go everywhere short of the abode of God.

12 *the concave compass of the pole:* i.e., the concave outer limits of all that revolves upon the axis of the universe.

24 *holy Peter's feast:* St Peter's day, 29 June.

SCENE viii

2 *Trier:* A city in western Germany, famous for its antiquities.

3 *Environ'd round with airy mountain-tops:* Trier is situated in a valley shut in by vine-clad hills.

7 *We saw the river Main fall into Rhine:* at Mainz.

9 *Naples, rich Campania:* The *Damnable Life*, here misrepresenting the original German, seems to have betrayed Marlowe into this erroneous identification of Campania with Naples.

12 *Quarters:* The third person plural in -s, as in vi, 20 and xviii, 125–6.

13–15 Publius Vergilius Maro, the author of the *Aeneid*, died in 19 B.C. and was buried at Naples in southern Italy. During the Middle Ages, Virgil acquired a surprising reputation as a necromancer, and an ancient passageway running through the promontory of Posillipo between Naples and Pozzuoli was ascribed to his arts.

17–20 This 'temple' is St Mark's, Venice. It has not, in fact, the 'aspiring top' which Marlowe here attributes to it. In all probability, he simply fell back upon one of his favourite terms to describe a building which the *Damnable Life* told him was 'sumptuous'. See note on iii, 70.

30 *All's one:* 'It's all the same whether he will or not.'

31–46 The 'city of Rome' which belonged to the Admiral's men in 1598 was perhaps a backcloth for use at this point.

39–40 In reality, the bridge leads to the castle, which stands upon the bank of the Tiber. The *Damnable Life* seems to have misled Marlowe. See 'Introduction'.

42 *double cannons:* Probably cannons of very large calibre.

44 *complete:* Accented on the first syllable.

45 *pyramides:* The obelisk which the Emperor Caligula brought from Heliopolis in Egypt in the first century A.D. and which was moved to the Piazza San Pietro, where it still stands, in 1586.

47–51 Styx, Acheron, and Phlegethon were supposed to be the three rivers of Hades, though one of them is here called a 'lake'. After Faustus has solemnly and emphatically sworn by them, it comes as a shock to learn that he longs for nothing more extraordinary than a sightseeing tour of Rome! Marlowe was by no means incapable of lapsing into such an anticlimax. But it is at about this point that most students of *Doctor Faustus* believe that Marlowe's hand disappears from the play (apart from Chorus 2) until scene xviii.

53–6 These lines echo the last three lines of Chorus 1.

57 *the Pope's triumphant victory:* See note on ll. 90–6.

69–75 A reference to the travels described in the first fourteen lines of Chorus I.

89 Stage-direction: *pillars:* Carried as symbols of dignity or office. The sixteenth-century Cardinal Wolsey, followed by Pole, seems to have substituted a pair of these portable pillars for the silver mace to which he had a right. The playwright transfers the usage to Rome.

90–6 Pope Adrian's victory over the imperial forces and his treatment of the captured Bruno, the rival pope elected by the Emperor, seem to have been suggested by passages in John Foxe's *Acts and Monuments,* better known as Foxe's Book of Martyrs. From this, the playwright could have learned how Adrian IV (1154–9) came into conflict with the Empire, 'blustering and thundering against Frederick, the emperor'. After his account of Adrian IV, Foxe continues: 'Although this Adrian was bad enough, yet came the next much worse, one Alexander III, who yet was not elected alone; for beside him the emperor, with nine cardinals, ... did set up another pope, named Victor IV. Between these two popes arose a foul schism and great discord.' Eventually Alexander, having captured Frederick's son, forced the Emperor to submit. Frederick was ordered to kneel at the Pope's feet. 'The proud pope, setting his foot upon the emperor's neck, said the verse of the psalm, "Super aspidem et basiliscum ambulabis, et conculcabis leonem et draconem:" that is, "Thou shalt walk upon the adder and on the basilisk, and shalt tread down the lion and the dragon." To whom the emperor answering again, said, "Non tibi sed Petro:" that is, "Not to thee, but to Peter." The pope again, "Et mihi et Petro;" "Both to me and to Peter." The emperor ... held his peace.' This is apparently the source both of the present passage – though there is a similar incident in 1 *Tamburlaine,* IV, ii – and of ll. 136–42.

99–100 The Pope refers to the proverb, 'God comes with leaden (woollen) feet but strikes with iron hands.'

104, 114 *consistory:* i.e., the meeting-place of the papal consistory or senate.

105 *statutes decretal:* This term is applied here to the whole of ecclesiastical law, including the decrees of councils.

106 *council held at Trent:* This council of the Roman Catholic
Church inaugurated the Counter-Reformation. It sat with inter-
ruptions from 1545 to 1563. This means that, like the reign of
Philip II (see note on i, 131), it opened after the death of the
historical Faustus (*c.* 1540).

112 *Lord Raymond* – While the Pope engages in private conversation with Raymond, Faustus, whose presence is unsuspected,
gives his instructions to Mephostophilis.

125 *let me have some right of law:* 'allow that I have some legal claim'.

126 *I was elected by the Emperor:* Bruno's reply to the charge that he
has assumed 'the papal government /Without election' (ll. 108–9).

127–31 Early in 1570, Pope Pius V issued a famous bull declaring
that Queen Elizabeth I was excommunicated, depriving her of
her right to the throne, and commanding her people, on pain of
anathema, to cease to obey her. This may well have been in the
playwright's mind.

129 *shalt:* Of the two subjects, 'he' and 'thou', the second has evidently been allowed to dictate the form of this verb.

136–42 See note on ll. 90–6.

142 *basilisk:* A fabulous reptile, also called a cockatrice, which was
said to be hatched by a serpent from a cock's egg and to be able
to kill by its look.

143 *schismatic:* Accented on the first and third syllables (and so in
l. 176 and in ix, 42).

146–8 This is fictitious. There was no Pope Julius during the lifetime of the Emperor Sigismund.

154 *keys:* of St Peter.

164 *consistory:* See note on ll. 104, 114.

176 *lollards:* This name was given to the followers of Wyclif and to
others holding similar heretical views.

182 *statutes decretal:* See note on l. 105.

186 *to Ponte Angelo:* i.e., to the castle which stands on (or by) the
bridge. See note on ll. 39–40.

188 *consistory:* See note on ll. 104, 114.

189 *college of grave cardinals:* The assembled cardinals of the Roman
Catholic Church, who constitute the Pope's council.

191 *his:* Bruno had assumed the tiara.

193 *again:* i.e., to return.

SCENE ix

Stage-direction: *in their own shapes:* i.e., no longer disguised as cardinals.

8 *his crown:* The 'triple crown' (viii, 191), which the Pope had ordered the bogus cardinals to deposit in the church's treasury.

19 *The planets seven:* listed in vi, 53–5.

20 *the Furies' forked hair:* The forked tongues of the snakes that are shown as forming the hair of the Furies.

21 *Pluto's blue fire:* The sulphurous flames associated with the god of the underworld.
Hecate's tree: Hecate was goddess of the infernal region, queen of night, ghosts, and magic, and guardian of witches. She was also the goddess of the cross-ways, so perhaps the gallows-tree is meant. Here, as in *Macbeth*, her name is disyllabic.

28 Stage-direction: *Lords:* including Raymond, King of Hungary, and the Archbishop of Rheims.

37 *consistory:* See note on viii, 104, 114.

59 *Fall to, the devil choke you an you spare:* 'Set to work, may the devil choke you if you hold back!' 'Fall to', meaning 'set to work, make a start', was used especially of eating. In vi, 158, Gluttony, refused an invitation to supper, curses Faustus with 'the devil choke thee'.

95 *this soul:* i.e., the 'troublesome ghost' (l. 86).

97 *cursed with bell, book, and candle:* This refers to a form of excommunication at the end of which the bell was tolled, the book closed, and the candle extinguished.

99 Stage-direction: *dirge:* Here used, less appropriately than in l. 85, to refer to the formal curse which follows. The word is used again in the same sense in l. 108.

103 *Maledicat Dominus:* 'May the Lord curse him.'

106 *took Friar Sandelo a blow on the pate:* This was presumably done during the dirge; the victim's name was evidently suggested by the sandals worn by friars.

112 *Et omnes sancti:* 'And all the saints'.

SCENE X

1–2 *we were best look that your devil can answer:* 'we had better make sure that your devil can justify'.

22 *Never outface me for the matter:* 'Don't try to brazen the matter out with me.'

24 *beyond us both:* i.e., out of our hands. Robin has now disposed of it.

27 *Ay, much!* A derisive exclamation, conveying incredulity.
when, can you tell? A defiant retort.
circle: i.e., magician's circle.

29 *Say nothing:* because speech is dangerous in the presence of spirits. Faustus gives a similar warning to the Emperor Charles V when he shows him Alexander and his Paramour and to the Scholars when he shows them Helen of Troy. See xii, 44–8 and xviii, 27.

30 *O per se, o; Demogorgon:* This echoes Robin's attempts to read from Faustus' conjuring book in vii, 7–8.
Belcher: One of the devils summoned by Wagner in iv, 32–8.

32–4 Mephostophilis makes it clear that the charms recited by Robin have brought him against his will from as far as Constantinople. But in iii, 46–56 he emphasized that the charms recited by Faustus had not compelled him to appear but had merely made him aware of Faustus' attractively sinful frame of mind, with the result that he had come of his own accord. The flat contradiction between these two views of the potency of the charms leads to the suspicion that if Marlowe wrote scene iii someone else must have written scene x.

50–1 *with the flames of ever-burning fire / I'll wing myself:* 'I'll make wings for myself from the flames of ever-burning fire.'

CHORUS 2

14 *Carolus the Fifth:* Charles V. See notes on Dramatis Personae, 13, and i, 131.

SCENE xi

13 *progenitors:* Here the meaning may be either 'predecessors', as in viii, 136, or 'ancestors', the more usual sense.

22 Stage-direction: *Enter Benvolio above at a window, in his nightcap, buttoning:* Benvolio appears at a window adjacent to the upper stage. He seems to have been roused from sleep. Still wearing his nightcap, he is buttoning up his clothes as he stares down from his bedroom to find the cause of the disturbance.

23 *What a devil ail you two?* 'What the devil's the matter with you two?'

30–2 *such rare exploits . . . | As never yet was seen:* The author must have considered the subject-noun 'exploits' as singular in thought, that is, as equivalent to some such term as 'performance'.

31 *Pope:* In the scenes at the Emperor's court, this naturally means Bruno.

SCENE xii

11 *despite of chance:* i.e., in spite of the bad luck that he has suffered.

44–8 A similar warning to those given by Robin in x, 29 and by Faustus himself in xviii, 27.

50 *And thou bring:* In Elizabethan English, the subjunctive is found, more frequently than in modern English, with 'if' (or 'and'), 'though', etc. Compare vi, 83.

51 *Actaeon:* He came upon Diana and her nymphs bathing. The goddess punished him for his intrusion by changing him into a stag, with the result that his own dogs tore him to pieces.

53 Stage-direction: *offering to go out:* i.e., Alexander offering (or proposing) to leave.

64 *prove that saying to be true:* 'put the truth of that statement to the test'.

70 *strange beast:* Benvolio has fallen asleep at his window, and Faustus' charms have caused a pair of horns to sprout from his head. The text of the scene does not enable us to say just how this was done on the stage, apparently in full view of the audience. What is clear, however, is that the play was written for performance by a highly skilled company in a well-equipped theatre.

79 *A plague upon you !* Benvolio has not yet recognized the Emperor.

80 *I blame thee not to sleep much:* 'I do not much blame you for sleeping.'

83–9 Benvolio's horns prevent him from pulling his head back through the window.

84 *and thy horns hold, 'tis no matter for thy head:* 'if your horns remain fast, it doesn't matter about your head.'

91 *these lords:* i.e., to these lords.

94–5 *straight resolv'd | In bold Actaeon's shape to turn a stag:* See ll. 50–2. Hence the appropriateness of the horns.

100 *Belimote, Argiron, Asterote:* The first and third of these devils'
names recur as Belimoth and Asteroth in xiii, 78. Belimoth is
perhaps derived from Behemoth, an animal mentioned in Job xl,
15–24, probably a hippopotamus; Asteroth is evidently Ashtaroth
or Astarte, the eastern equivalent of the Greek Aphrodite, the
goddess of love and fruitful increase. Argiron is more puzzling
but is possibly a perversion of Acheron.

114 *cuckold-makers:* An allusion to the old and widespread belief
that cuckolds sprouted horns. See note on vii, 19.

115 *smooth faces and small ruffs:* i.e., beardless scholars in academical
garb.

117–18 *drink nothing but salt water:* This would be a particularly
dreadful fate for Benvolio, of whom we first heard when he was
sleeping off the effects of having taken 'his rouse with stoups of
Rhenish wine' (xi, 18).

SCENE xiii

37 Stage-direction: *the false head:* The author asks for *the* false head
which he knew the company to possess or knew that it would
acquire. Presumably the 'gown' (l. 34) worn by Faustus makes it
easier for the actor to hide his true head. Fitted up in this way,
he will be able to undergo an innocuous decapitation at l. 44.

71–2 *limited | For four-and-twenty years:* 'accorded the fixed period
of twenty-four years'.

78 *Asteroth, Belimoth:* For these names, see note on xii, 100.

94 *He must needs go that the devil drives:* A well-known proverb.
Stage-direction: *the ambushed Soldiers:* who left the stage at l. 25.

105 Stage-direction: *the door:* of the stage. The imagined setting is
a wood.

SCENE xiv

4–5 In Shakespeare's *Merry Wives of Windsor*, probably written in
1600–1, Bardolph apparently compares his own sufferings with
those of these three knights: 'so soon as I came beyond Eton, they
threw me off, from behind one of them, in a slough of mire; and
set spurs and away, like three German devils, three Doctor
Faustuses' (IV, v, 65–9).

6 *Benvolio's:* Benvolio has.

9 *Nay, fear not, man, we have no power to kill:* Martino plays upon
   'haunted' and 'hunted'. Benvolio has asked, 'shall I be haunted
   still ?' (l. 8). Martino replies that though Benvolio has been partly
   transformed into animal likeness the others are not equipped for
   hunting him to death.

15 *doubled:* A trisyllable.

25 *We'll rather die with grief than live with shame:* A variant of the
   proverb, 'It is better to die with honour than to live with shame.'

SCENE XV

Stage-direction: *Horse-courser:* A horse-dealer had a ready-made
   reputation for dishonesty. So an audience would be very ready
   to applaud Faustus' humiliation of one, despite the fact that the
   Horse-courser differs from Benvolio in not having given any
   particular offence to Faustus.

13–14 *will he not drink of all waters ?* 'Will he not be ready for anything ?'

21–6 Faustus' first expression of misgivings since before the show
   of the Seven Deadly Sins.

24 *Confound these passions:* 'Disperse these agitating emotions.'

33–4 *your horse is turned to a bottle of hay:* Dryden refers to this
   transformation in his play *An Evening's Love*, III, i: 'A witch's
   horse, you know, when he enters into water, returns into a bottle
   of hay again.'

40–1 *Faustus hath his leg again:* A new leg has magically replaced
   that stolen by the Horse-courser.

48 *I must be no niggard of my cunning:* 'I must not be a miser with
   my skill.'

SCENE XVI

2 *Where be these whores ?* A coarse summons to the Hostess and her
   staff.

11–13 Robin hopes that his debt stands 'still', i.e., 'without increasing'. The Hostess gives 'still' another meaning, i.e., 'always', and
   retorts that he is in no hurry to pay what he owes her.

15 *You shall presently. Look up into th' hall there, ho !* The Hostess
   assures them that they will have their beer without delay; then
   she calls out an instruction to her staff.

18 *Marry:* An exclamation, derived from the name of the Virgin Mary.

19 *Fauster:* A clownish corruption of 'Faustus' (and so in l. 38).

20 *Here's some on's have:* 'There are some of us here who have'.

28 *cursen:* A dialectal form of 'christen', i.e., 'Christian'.

28, 31 *eat:* 'eaten'. Elizabethan authors often use such curtailed forms of past participles as this. Compare 'He has forgot' (xvii, 76).

31–2 *that has eat a load of logs:* Not yet satisfactorily explained. Perhaps it means, 'who has wastefully consumed the timber standing on his estate'.

51 *now 'tis at home in mine hostry:* It appears that the Horse-courser did not carry out his intention of casting the leg 'into some ditch or other' (xv, 39).

53–4 *turned me into the likeness of an ape's face:* in scene x.

SCENE xvii

27–30 The 'two circles' ought to have been defined as the northern and southern hemispheres. Instead, the dramatist muddles the account by distinguishing between a western circle and one containing 'India, Saba, and such countries that lie far east'.

30 *Saba:* Sheba. Compare v, 157.

41 *a fig for him !* An expression of contempt. By his charms, Faustus has brought the clowns into close proximity with the Duke without disturbing their belief that they are merely passing into 'another room' (xvi, 56) in the tavern.

43–4 *I hope, sir, we have wit enough to be more bold than welcome:* The Horse-courser thinks that in a tavern a man ought to get a better welcome than he and his friends are receiving. He hopes that they have sense enough to behave with a boldness that will more than make up for the poor hospitality shown them.

45 *It appears so:* 'That is obvious.' The Servant knows that they are not in the least welcome.

49–51 The Duke means, 'Take the rascals to prison'; but Dick gives 'commit' the meaning 'have sexual intercourse'.

58–9 *we will be welcome for our money, and we will pay for what we take:* Convinced that he is in a tavern, Robin insists that they will pay for their welcome.

63 *sir sauce-box:* A name given to a person who makes saucy or impertinent remarks.

71 *Our servants and our court's at thy command:* The Duke is placing both his 'servants' and his 'court' at Faustus' command. The verb has been allowed to take the number of the subject immediately preceding it.

73 *marry:* An exclamation, derived from the name of the Virgin Mary.

76 *forgot:* See note on xvi, 28, 31.

77 *stand much upon:* 'attach much importance to'. In his reply, Faustus exploits the literal meaning of the words.

88–90 The Carter's word 'curtsy' brings out a second meaning of 'leg' (l. 86), i.e., 'obeisance, bow'. In response, Faustus makes him a polite bow, accompanying it ironically with the words, 'I thank you, sir.' To this, the Carter replies, with self-conscious courtesy, ''Tis not so much worth,' i.e., 'Don't mention it.'

93–4 *Wouldst thou make a colossus of me, that thou askest me such questions?* 'If you really doubt whether my legs are "bedfellows every night together" (l. 92), you must think me capable of separating them so widely that I become like the Colossus of Rhodes. There can be no other explanation of your asking me such questions.' The Colossus of Rhodes passed for one of the seven wonders of the ancient world, and its legs were commonly, though erroneously, said to have straddled the harbour entrance so that ships passed between them.

95 *make nothing of:* The Carter uses the words not only in the literal sense but also colloquially to mean 'make light of'.

109 *whoreson:* A coarsely abusive epithet. The literal meaning, when the word is used as a noun, is 'whore's son'.

112 *'hey-pass'* and *'re-pass':* Exclamations employed by jugglers and conjurors when commanding articles to move. The similar term 'hey presto' is more familiar today.

114 *Who pays for the ale?* which she brought in at l. 96.

SCENE xviii

15 *that favour, as to:* 'such a favour as to'.

15–17 *that peerless dame of Greece, whom all the world admires for majesty:* These words anticipate ll. 23 and 29.

25 *Sir:* This title assimilates Paris to a hero of mediaeval romance. Compare l. 109.

26 *the spoils:* The booty, including Helen, acquired during his expedition to Sparta.
  Dardania: Troy. Poets often refer to it, as here, by the name of the city which Dardanus built upon the Hellespont.

27 *Be silent, then, for danger is in words:* A similar warning to those given by Robin in x, 29 and by Faustus himself in xii, 44–8.

27 Stage-direction: *she passeth over the stage:* Helen enters the yard or pit of the theatre, walks to the stage, mounts on to it by steps set for the purpose, crosses it, descends, and leaves by the yard or pit on the other side. Many Elizabethan stage-directions speak of 'passing over the stage', and this seems the likeliest explanation of the phrase.

31 *ten years' war:* The siege of Troy.

37 Stage-direction: *Enter an Old Man:* The Old Man is almost as much of a morality-play character as the Good and Bad Angels or the various evil spirits. There would be little or no inappropriateness in re-naming him Good Counsel.

42 *persever:* Accented on the second syllable.

43–4 'You have still a soul that is worthy of love so long as sin does not by habit become natural to you.'

56 Stage-direction: *Mephostophilis gives him a dagger:* In Spenser's *Faerie Queene*, I, ix, 29, Despair gives a 'rustie knife' and a 'rope' to two intended victims. The same symbolic temptation occurs in *A Looking-Glass for London and England*, a play by Thomas Lodge and Robert Greene.

77 *I do repent I e'er offended him:* The opening words of this line ironically echo those of l. 71. In the earlier line, Faustus strives to repent his abjuring of God but despairs of the divine mercy. In the later line, his 'repentance' has taken the opposite direction; he repents that he has ever wavered in his loyalty to evil.

98 Stage-direction: *passing over:* Helen walks from the yard or pit, across the stage, and out by the yard on the other side. Her Cupids accompany her, and Faustus leaves with them at the end of his speech. See note on l. 27.

99 *launch'd a thousand ships:* i.e., caused a thousand Greek ships to be launched for the siege of Troy. In 2 *Tamburlaine*, II, iv, 87–8,

Marlowe has: 'Helen, whose beauty summoned Greece to arms, /
And drew a thousand ships to Tenedos'.

100 *Ilium:* Troy.

105 Stage-direction: *Enter Old Man:* Faustus' elated surrender of
himself to the diabolical 'semblance' (xi, 15) of Helen of Troy is
to be witnessed by the representative of the orthodoxy which
condemns it.

108 *I will combat with weak Menelaus:* Homer describes how Menelaus, the husband of Helen, would have defeated Paris in single
combat but for the intervention of the goddess Aphrodite (*Iliad*,
iii).

109 *wear thy colours on my plumed crest:* like a mediaeval knight.
Compare l. 25.

110 *in the heel:* This was the only place where the Greek hero
Achilles was vulnerable. According to a non-Homeric story, he
was killed by an arrow, shot by Paris, which struck his heel.

115 *Semele:* She asked Zeus to visit her in his divine splendour and
was consumed by his lightning.

116–17 'More beautiful than the sun when it is reflected in the blue
waters of the spring Arethusa'. Marlowe does not seem to be
thinking of any specific incident in classical mythology.

118 *none but thou shalt:* Marlowe has allowed 'thou' rather than
'none' to dictate the form of the verb.

125–6 *smiles . . . laughs:* The third person plural in -s, as in vi, 20
and viii, 12.

127 *I fly unto my God:* It is not certain whether the Old Man's faith
gives him physical immunity or a martyr's spiritual victory. In
either case, he triumphs over hell. If the dramatist followed the
Damnable Life, the Old Man was physically unharmed. See 'Introduction'.

SCENE xix

Stage-direction: *Enter Lucifer, Beelzebub, and Mephostophilis above:*
As in scene iii, in which Faustus first invoked the powers of evil,
diabolical characters watch what he does without being seen by
him. Presumably they stand upon the upper stage.

1 *Dis:* A name sometimes given to Pluto, the god of the underworld,
and hence also, as here, to the regions over which he ruled.

28 *chamber-fellow:* It was customary in the Elizabethan period for two or more university students to occupy the same room.

30 *comes he not? comes he not?* Faustus knows that the time has almost arrived when, as he says in l. 144, 'The devil will come, and Faustus must be damn'd'.

36 *a surfeit:* An illness caused by excessive eating or drinking, such as killed the playwright Robert Greene in 1592.

71-2 *the devil threatened to tear me in pieces if I named God:* In vi, 83, the Bad Angel threatens, 'If thou repent, devils will tear thee in pieces'; and in xviii, 76, Mephostophilis commands, 'Revolt, or I'll in piecemeal tear thy flesh'.

87 *Meph.:* During the conversation between Faustus and the Scholars, Mephostophilis has descended from the upper stage, leaving Lucifer and Beelzebub there. He now confronts his victim.

96 *led thine eye:* for example, to the texts juxtaposed in i, 39-43.

105 Stage-direction: *the throne:* This could be let down from the theatrical 'heavens' by means of cords and pulleys. In his Prologue to *Every Man in his Humour*, Ben Jonson refers disparagingly to plays in which a 'creaking throne comes down the boys to please'. In the present scene, the throne represents that which Faustus might have occupied in heaven.

111 *sit:* This form of the past participle is found elsewhere in Elizabethan writing.

115 Stage-direction: *Exit. Hell is discovered:* The throne is raised and the Good Angel retires. The horrors of hell are then suggested either by the Bad Angel's drawing a curtain and so revealing a painted backcloth or by the use of a trap uncovered with smoke etc. arising.

120 *quarters:* of human bodies, as in the case of those executed for treason.

121 *That:* i.e., the quarters.

123 *sops:* Normally, pieces of cake or the like soaked in a prepared drink; here, soaked in 'flaming fire'.

132 Stage-direction: *Exit:* The Bad Angel retires either behind the curtain, drawing it so as to conceal both himself and the painted backcloth representing hell, or by way of the trap. Lucifer and Beelzebub still watch Faustus from above.

135 *And then thou must be damn'd perpetually:* This line has been carefully prepared for. It is anticipated in l. 102, 'And now must taste hell's pains perpetually', and its key term, the word which focuses Faustus' dread, has been kept in our minds by the reference to the 'perpetual torture-house' in l. 117. Nor is the word now to be forgotten. It recurs in l. 139.

142 *O lente lente currite noctis equi:* 'Run slowly, slowly, O horses of the night.' Faustus quotes from Ovid, *Amores*, I, xiii, 40. The quotation has ironical implications, for, whereas Ovid wishes to prolong the night he is spending with his lover, Faustus wishes merely to postpone the anguish of the morrow.

146 *See, see where Christ's blood streams in the firmament:* T. S. Eliot points to this as a triumphantly successful remodelling of Marlowe's earlier line, 'And set black streamers in the firmament' (2 *Tamburlaine*, V, iii, 49).

148 *Rend not my heart for naming of my Christ:* Already Faustus has called on Christ in vi, 85–6 and has striven to do so again in xviii, 71. On each occasion, the devils have made him suffer for his violation of his vow and have halted his movement towards repentance. The same process is now repeated once more.

150 *Where is it now? 'Tis gone:* The movement towards repentance ended with the cry, 'O, spare me, Lucifer!' (l. 149). Because he has thus called on Lucifer, Faustus now loses the vision of Christ's blood.

152–3 Compare Revelation vi, 16: 'And said to the mountains and rocks, Fall on us, and hide us from the face of him that sitteth on the throne, and from the wrath of the Lamb.' See also Hosea x, 8.

153 *the heavy wrath of God:* The first speech of the Good Angel warned Faustus against incurring 'God's heavy wrath' (i, 71).

157–63 Faustus implores the planets which were dominant at the time of his birth, and on to which he would like to shift the responsibility for his damnation, to draw him up in vapour into a cloud. There his gross earthly parts (his 'limbs') would be consolidated into a thunderstone and rejected, leaving his purified soul fit for admission into heaven. Marlowe is here using current meteorological notions.

158 *influence:* The supposed streaming from the stars of an ethereal fluid acting upon the characters and destiny of men.

161–2 Grammatically, 'you' and 'your' should refer to 'stars' (l. 157), but the sense demands that they refer to the nearer substantive, 'cloud' (l. 160). Psychologically, it is appropriate that Faustus' appeal should shift from one to the other of the physical agents of the purification he dreams of.

164 *Ah, half the hour is pass'd: 'twill all be pass'd anon:* This alexandrine, with its marked internal pause, is tellingly expressive of Faustus' agony in his last speech; and the same may be said of the earlier alexandrine at l. 147. See note on v, 6–7.

174 *Pythagoras' metempsychosis:* Pythagoras of Samos, who flourished in the sixth century B.C., was regarded as the author of the doctrine of the transmigration of souls from one body to another.

181–2 *curse Lucifer / That hath depriv'd thee of the joys of heaven:* These words ironically echo Faustus' arrogant reproof to the suffering Mephostophilis in iii, 85–6: 'What, is great Mephostophilis so passionate / For being deprived of the joys of heaven?'

190 *books:* of magic.
Ah, Mephostophilis: Mephostophilis, who left Faustus at l. 98, has evidently reappeared as one of the Devils that are to drag him away.
Stage-direction: *Exeunt with him:* The hell to which the Devils drag Faustus could be either behind a curtain at the rear of the stage or below the stage. See note on the stage-direction at l. 115.

SCENE XX

6 *here are Faustus' limbs:* Perhaps the Second Scholar draws back the curtain and so discovers Faustus' remains.

EPILOGUE

1 *Cut is the branch that might have grown full straight:* Marlowe evidently allowed this moving line to be suggested to him by a line written by a minor contemporary, Thomas Churchyard: 'bent the wand that might have grown full straight'.

2 *Apollo's laurel bough:* The emblem of distinction in poetry, etc. Apollo was the god of song and of learning.

6 *Only to wonder:* 'To be content with merely wondering'.
Motto: *Terminat hora diem; terminat Author opus:* 'The hour ends the day; the author ends his work.' This may have been added by the printer. 'Auctor' would be better Latin than 'Author', but the motto was current in the form here used.

Short Bibliography

EDITIONS OF MARLOWE'S WORKS

The Works and Life of Christopher Marlowe, ed. R. H. Case, 6 vols., London, 1930–3.

Marlowe's 'Doctor Faustus': 1604–1616, ed. W. W. Greg, Oxford, 1950.

Doctor Faustus, ed. J. D. Jump, London, 1962. (The Revels Plays.)

BIOGRAPHICAL STUDIES

J. Bakeless, *Christopher Marlowe*, London, 1938.

F. S. Boas, *Christopher Marlowe: A Biographical and Critical Study*, Oxford, 1940.

CRITICAL STUDIES

J. P. Brockbank, *Marlowe: Dr. Faustus*, London, 1962.

P. H. Kocher, *Christopher Marlowe: A Study of his Thought, Learning, and Character*, Chapel Hill, 1946.

H. Levin, *The Overreacher*, London, 1954.

J. B. Steane, *Marlowe: A Critical Study*, Cambridge, 1964.

See also the essays by T. S. Eliot (in *Selected Essays*, London, 1932); by M. M. Mahood (in *Poetry and Humanism*, London, 1950); and by J. C. Maxwell (in *The Pelican Guide to English Literature* (ed. B. Ford), ii: *The Age of Shakespeare*, 1955).

Essays, and extracts from longer studies, are reprinted in Marlowe, *Doctor Faustus: A Casebook*, ed. John Jump, London, 1969.